HERE WE STAND
STUDENT BOOK

HERE WE STAND
STUDENT BOOK

To Justin,

For Confirmation on
May 6, 2018
Hope this guides you!
Love,
Grandma Joan

Augsburg Fortress

Minneapolis

Scripture quotations are from the New Revised Standard Version Bible, copyright © 1989, Division of Christian Education of the National Council of the Churches of Christ in the United States of America.

Pages 176–81: Sources for the charts include reference materials from *Information Please*,® New York Times Public Library/Hyperion, Rose Publishing, Time-Life, and Wadsworth Group/Thomas Learning.

Pages 312–20: Glossary reprinted from *Altar Guild and Sacristy Handbook*, by S. Anita Stauffer, copyright © 2000 Augsburg Fortress.

Pages 296–311: Translation of Luther's Small Catechism from *The Book of Concord*, Robert Kolb and Timothy J. Wengert, eds. © 2000 Augsburg Fortress. All rights reserved. This altered version is from *Evangelical Lutheran Worship*.

Cover design: Joe Vaughan
Interior design: Joe Vaughan
Interior illustrator: Brenda Brown

Contributing writers: Rod Anderson, Chip Borgstadt, Ramona S. Bouzard, Walter C. Bouzard, Suzanne Burke, Eric Burtness, Louis R. Carlozo, Carol Carver, Giacomo Cassese, Chris Duckworth, Mark Gardner, Wes Halula, Rod Hank, Paul N. Hanson, Sarah Henrich, Mark Hinton, Susan Houglum, Mark J. Jackson, Rolf A. Jacobson, Mark D. Johns, Mark K. Johnson, Ken Sundet Jones, James Kasperson, Timothy Keyl, Charles R. Lane, Susan M. Lang, Andrea Lee, Daniel Levitin, Catherine Malotky, Terry Marks, Mark C. Mattes, Sally Messner, Jennifer Moland-Kovash, Seth Moland-Kovash, Jeffrey S. Nelson, Rebecca Ninke, Marc Ostlie-Olson, Paul Owens, Eliseo Pérez-Álvarez, Dawn Rundman, Jonathan Rundman, Ted Schroeder, Tom Teichmann, Megan J. Thorvilson, Megan Torgerson, Erik Ullestad, Darin Wiebe, Hans Wiersma, and Steven Zittergruen

ISBN 978-0-8066-9845-8
The paper used in this publication meets the minimum requirements of American National Standard for Information Sciences—Permanence of Paper for Printed Library Materials, ANSI Z329.48-1984.

19 18 17   7 8 9 10

CONTENTS

MAPS AND DIAGRAMS

CHURCH STUFF 121

MAPS AND DIAGRAMS

EVERYDAY STUFF 187

SMALL CATECHISM OF
MARTIN LUTHER   295

THIS BOOK BELONGS TO

Name_____

Address_____

_____

Telephone_____

Email_____

Birth date_____

Baptismal birth date_____

First communion_____

Confirmation date_____

Godparents' (baptismal sponsors') names

_____

_____

_____

_____

Churches I've belonged to:	Years of membership
_____	_____
_____	_____
_____	_____
_____	_____
_____	_____
_____	_____

ABOUT MY CONGREGATION

Name_____

Address_____

_____

Year organized/founded_____

My pastor(s) _____

_____

_____

_____

Number of baptized members_____

Average weekly worship attendance_____

Facts about my denomination_____

_____

_____

_____

Other information about my congregation and faith

_____

_____

_____

_____

BIBLE STUFF

Written down by many people over hundreds of years, the Bible is more like a portable bookshelf than one book by itself. And because the Bible is God's Word, people often feel overwhelmed when they try to read it.

This section includes:

] Helpful information about when, where, and why people wrote the 66 books within the Bible. (It didn't all come together at once.)

] Tips for reading and understanding the Bible—how it's organized and what it says.

] Some of the most mystifying, hair-raising, and just plain off-the-wall stories in the Bible.

A BRIEF HISTORY OF THE BIBLE

A smaller number in B.C.E. (Before Common Era) time actually denotes a year that is later in history than the larger number. For example, events in 1500 B.C.E. happened after events that occurred in 1700 B.C.E. With C.E. (Common Era) dates, on the other hand, the years get progressively larger. The dates below are approximates.

CREATION.
God created the universe and everything in it; the things God created continue to create and procreate.

1700–1500 B.C.E. THE ANCESTORS.
God blesses Abraham and Sarah and their descendants so that they will in turn bless the rest of the world.

1240 B.C.E. THE EXODUS.
God hears the groans of the people in Egypt and frees them from Pharaoh's slavery.

1240–1200 B.C.E. SINAI AND WILDERNESS.
God makes a covenant with the people at Mount Sinai and gives them laws, such as the Ten Commandments.

1200 B.C.E. THE LAND.
God gives the people a land to live in.

1200–1000 B.C.E. PERIOD OF THE JUDGES.
God serves as the "King" of the twelve tribes of Israel so that they don't have to live under a human king. Leaders, known as "judges," serve as the human leaders under God's rule.

1000 B.C.E. THE UNITED MONARCHY.
The people want to be like other nations, so they demand a human king. Saul becomes Israel's first human king.

960 B.C.E. DAVID.

God promises David that one of his descendants will forever be king of Israel; David moves the capital to Jerusalem.

940 B.C.E. TEMPLE.

Solomon builds God a temple in Jerusalem.

922 B.C.E. THE DIVIDED MONARCHY.

The nation splits in half because of bad leadership. The northern kingdom is called "Israel" and the southern kingdom is called "Judah."

922–722 B.C.E. NORTHERN KINGDOM.

Israel lasts until Assyria destroys it in 722 B.C.E. Its capital is Samaria; its descendants are called Samaritans.

922–587 B.C.E. SOUTHERN KINGDOM.

Judah lasts until Babylon destroys Jerusalem and its temple in 587 B.C.E. Its descendants are called Jews. During these years, first editions of many books of the Old Testament are written.

587–539 B.C.E. EXILE AND DIASPORA.*

The leaders of the people live in Babylon in exile until Babylon is conquered and they can return home. Many of them never return home, so God's people spread out across the world.

520–450 B.C.E. REBUILDING JUDEA.

Some exiled people return and rebuild the temple and Jerusalem. The people are not their own nation, but a province of Persia. Many books of the Old Testament reach their final form during these years.

* "Diaspora" refers to the populations of Jews exiled from Judea in this time, who were disbursed to surrounding and neighboring lands.

330 B.C.E. GREEK RULE.
The Greeks conquer the Holy Land and rule Judea.

67 B.C.E. ROMAN RULE.
The Romans conquer the Holy Land and rule Judea. By this time, all of the books of the Old Testament are completed.

4 B.C.E. THE CHRIST.
Jesus Christ is born.

C.E. 26–29. JESUS' PUBLIC MINISTRY.
Jesus ministers, teaches, and preaches publicly. He calls his first followers.

C.E. 29. CRUCIFIXION AND RESURRECTION.
Jesus is crucified and raised from the dead.

C.E. 29. PENTECOST.
God sends the Holy Spirit and the church is born.

C.E. 35. PAUL'S CONVERSION.
Saul, a persecutor of the church, converts and becomes a leading evangelist.

C.E. 50–100. NEW TESTAMENT WRITTEN.
The documents that later became part of the New Testament are written.

In 67 B.C.E. the Romans conquered the Holy Land, but the Old Testament books had pretty much been completed by then anyway.

COMMON TRANSLATIONS OF THE BIBLE

Translation	Grade Level*	Theological Affiliation	Year Released	Special Features
King James Version	12.0	Church of England, conservative and evangelical	1611	Poetic style using Elizabethan English. Most widely used translation for centuries.
New American Standard Bible	11.0	Conservative and evangelical	1971; updated, 1995	Revision of the 1901 American Standard Version into contemporary language.
New Revised Standard Version	8.1	Mainline and interconfessional	1989	Updated version of the Revised Standard Version.
New King James Version	8.0	Transnational, transdenominational, conservative, and evangelical	1982	Updates the King James text into contemporary language.
New International Version	7.8	Transnational, transdenominational, conservative, and evangelical	1978; revised, 1984	Popular modern-language version. Attempts to balance literal and dynamic translation methods.
Today's English Version (also called the Good News Bible)	7.3	Evangelical and interconfessional	1976	Noted for its freshness of language.

Version	Grade level	Classification	Date	Description
New American Bible	6.6	Roman Catholic	1970; revised NT, 1986; revised Psalms, 1991	Official translation of the Roman Catholic Church in the United States.
New Living Translation	6.4	Evangelical	1996	A meaning-for-meaning translation. Successor to the Living Bible.
New Century Version	5.6	Conservative and evangelical	1988; revised, 1991	Follows the Living Word Vocabulary.
Contemporary English Version	5.4	Conservative, evangelical, mainline	1995	Easy-to-read English for new Bible readers.
The Message	4.8, from NT samples	Evangelical	2002	An expressive paraphrase of the Bible.

* The grade level on which the text is written, using Dale-chall, Fry, Raygor, and Spache Formulas.

BIBLE CLASSIFICATIONS

Apocrypha Bible: Contains certain books that Protestants don't consider canonical. Most of these OT books are accepted by the Roman Catholic Church.

Children's Bible: Includes illustrations and other study aids that are especially helpful for children.

Concordance Bible: Lists places in the Bible where key words are found.

Red Letter Bible: The words spoken by Christ appear in red.

Reference Bible: Pages include references to other Bible passages on the same subject.

Self-Proclaiming Bible: Diacritical marks (as in a dictionary) appear above difficult names and words to help with the pronunciation.

Text Bible: Contains text without footnotes or column references. May include maps, illustrations, and other helpful material.

HOW TO CHOOSE A BIBLE TRANSLATION THAT'S RIGHT FOR YOU

Unless you already read biblical Hebrew, Aramaic, and Greek, you need a Bible translation. You could go learn these languages, but someone's already done the work for you. Choose wisely to enjoy a lifetime relationship with the Scriptures.

1 **EXAMINE YOURSELF AND YOUR MOTIVATIONS.**
Think about who you are and why you want to explore the Bible. Do you need a simple Bible or a more nuanced translation? Is this Bible for devotional use or for in-depth study? Do you need one with lots of pictures and small words?

2 **CONSIDER A BIBLE PRINTED IN A LANGUAGE YOU ACTUALLY SPEAK.**
For example, if thou dost not maketh use of words like *dost* or *maketh*, picketh thou another translation.

3 **SEEK AN ACTUAL TRANSLATION, NOT A PARAPHRASED VERSION.**
A paraphrase is a rewording of the Bible, an interpretation of a translation. This is like making a photocopy of a photocopy; resolution and clarity start to diminish. Look on the title page or preface for a phrase like "translated from the original languages."

4 DETERMINE THE TRANSLATION'S LEVEL OF FAITHFULNESS TO THE ORIGINAL WORDING.

Look for footnotes offering alternative translations or that point out where the biblical texts are difficult and the meaning uncertain. Translators often make tough choices; good translations clue you in.

5 READ A FAMILIAR PASSAGE.

Can you understand what you are reading? Does it help you hear God's word anew? Consider a passage *other* than John 3:16.

Unless you can read biblical Hebrew, Aramaic, and Greek, you might want to find yourself a good translation in a language you understand.

BIBLE STUFF

6 CLARIFY YOUR NEED FOR "HELPS."

Does the translation include introductions and explanations by reputable scholars? Such comments are not a part of the Bible, but can be a real plus in understanding the text, especially for serious study. Some study Bibles use call-outs and discussion questions to add another interesting dimension to Scripture reading.

BE AWARE

] Jesus speaks to us through the Bible. Reading an accurate, understandable translation can result in radical life transformations, spiritual maturity, and actual growth in faith.

] Unless you actually carry your Bible around with you everywhere, do not purchase a nylon cover with zipper and pockets. They're geeky.

60 ESSENTIAL BIBLE STORIES

Story	Bible Text	Key Verse
1. Creation	Genesis 1–2	Genesis 1:27
2. The Human Condition	Genesis 3–4	Genesis 3:5
3. The Flood and the First Covenant	Genesis 6–9	Genesis 9:8
4. The Tower of Babel and Abraham and Sarah	Genesis 11–12	Genesis 12:1
5. Sarah, Hagar, and Abraham	Genesis 12–25	Genesis 17:19
6. Isaac and Rebecca	Genesis 22–25	Genesis 24:67
7. Jacob and Esau	Genesis 25–36	Genesis 28:15
8. Joseph and God's Hidden Ways	Genesis 37–50	Genesis 50:20
9. Moses and Pharaoh	Exodus 1–15	Exodus 2:23
10. The Ten Commandments	Exodus 20	Exodus 20:2
11. From the Wilderness into the Promised Land	Exodus 16–18; Deuteronomy 1–6; Joshua 1–3, 24	Deuteronomy 6:4
12. Judges	Book of Judges	Judges 21:25
13. Ruth	Book of Ruth	Ruth 4:14
14. Samuel and Saul	1 Samuel 1–11	1 Samuel 3:1
15. King David	multiple OT books	1 Samuel 8:6
16. David, Nathan, and What Is a Prophet?	2 Samuel 11–12	2 Samuel 7:12
17. Solomon	1 Kings 1–11	1 Kings 6:12
18. Split of the Kingdom	1 Kings 11–12	1 Kings 12:16
19. Northern Kingdom, Its Prophets and Fate	1 Kings—2 Kings 17	Amos 5:21
20. Southern Kingdom, Its Prophets and Fate (Part 1)	multiple OT books	Isaiah 5:7

Story	Bible Text	Key Verse
21. Southern Kingdom, Its Prophets and Fate (Part 2)	multiple OT books	Jeremiah 31:31
22. The Exile	Isaiah 40–55; Ezekiel	Isaiah 40:10
23. Return from Exile	multiple OT books	Ezra 1:1
24. Ezra and Nehemiah	Books of Ezra and Nehemiah	Ezra 3:10
25. Esther	Book of Esther	Esther 4:14
26. Job	Book of Job	Job 1:1
27. Daniel	Book of Daniel	Daniel 3:17
28. Psalms of Praise and Trust	Psalms 8, 30, 100, 113, 121	Psalm 121:1
29. Psalms for Help	various psalms	Psalm 22:1
30. Wisdom	Job, Proverbs, Ecclesiastes	Proverbs 1:7
31. The Annunciation	Luke 1:26-56	Luke 1:31-33
32. Magi	Matthew 2:1-12	Matthew 2:2-3
33. Birth of Jesus	Luke 2:1-20	Luke 2:10-11
34. Simeon	Luke 2:25-35	Luke 2:30-32
35. Wilderness Temptations	Matthew 4:1-11; Mark 1:12-13; Luke 4:1-13	Luke 4:12-13
36. Jesus' Nazareth Sermon	Matthew 13:54-58; Mark 6:1-6; Luke 4:16-30	Luke 4:18-19, 21
37. Jesus Calls the First Disciples	Matthew 4:18-22; Mark 1:16-20; Luke 5:1-11	Luke 5:9-10
38. Beatitudes	Matthew 5:3-12	Luke 6:20-26
39. Gerasene Demoniac	Matthew 8:28-34; Mark 5:1-20; Luke 8:26-39	Luke 8:39
40. Feeding of the 5,000	Matthew 14:13-21; Mark 6:30-44; Luke 9:10-17; John 6:1-14	Luke 9:16-17

Story	Bible Text	Key Verse
41. The Transfiguration	Matthew 17:1-8; Mark 9:2-8; Luke 9:28-36	Luke 9:34-35
42. Sending of the Seventy	Matthew 8:19-22; Luke 10:1-16	Luke 10:8, 16
43. Good Samaritan	Luke 10:25-37	Luke 10:27-28
44. Healing the Bent-Over Woman	Luke 13:10-17	Luke 13:16
45. Parables of Lost and Found	Luke 15:1-32	Luke 15:31-32
46. Rich Man and Lazarus	Luke 16:19-31	Luke 16:29-31
47. Zacchaeus	Luke 19:1-11	Luke 19:9
48. Sheep and Goats	Matthew 25:31-46	Matthew 25:40
49. Parable of the Vineyard	Matthew 21:33-46; Mark 12:1-12; Luke 20:9-19; (Isaiah 5:1-7)	Luke 20:14-16
50. The Last Supper	Matthew 26:20-29; Mark 14:12-16; Luke 22:14-38	Luke 22:19-20, 27
51. Crucifixion	Matthew 27; Mark 15; Luke 23; John 19	Luke 23:42-43, 46
52. Road to Emmaus	Luke 24	Luke 24:30-31
53. Pentecost	Acts 2:1-21	Acts 2:17-18
54. Healing the Lame Man	Acts 3–4	Acts 4:19
55. Baptism of the Ethiopian	Acts 8:26-39	Acts 8:35-37
56. Call of Saul	Acts 7:58—8:1; 9:1-30	Acts 9:15-16
57. Peter and Cornelius	Acts 10	Acts 10:34-35
58. Philippians Humility	Philippians 2:1-13	Philippians 2:12-13
59. Love Hymn	1 Corinthians 13	1 Corinthians 13:4-7
60. Resurrection	1 Corinthians 15	1 Corinthians 15:51-55

HOW TO READ THE BIBLE

The Bible is a collection of 66 separate books gathered together over hundreds of years and thousands of miles. Divided into the Old Testament (Hebrew language) and the New Testament (Greek language), these writings have many authors and take many forms.

The Bible includes histories, stories, prophecies, poetry, songs, teachings, and laws, to name a few. Christians believe the Bible is the story of God's relationship with humankind and a powerful way that God speaks to people.

1 **DETERMINE YOUR PURPOSE FOR READING.**
   Clarify in your own mind what you hope to gain. Your motivations should be well intentioned, such as to seek information, to gain a deeper understanding of God and yourself, or to enrich your faith. Pray for insight before every reading time.

2 **RESOLVE TO READ DAILY.**
   Commit to a daily regimen of Bible reading. Make it a part of your routine until it becomes an unbreakable habit.

Commit to reading the Bible daily.

3 MASTER THE MECHANICS.

- Memorize the books of the Bible in order.

- Familiarize yourself with the introductory material. Many Bible translations include helpful information at the front of the Bible and at the beginning of each book.

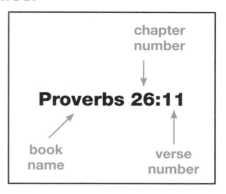

- The books are broken down into chapters and verses. Locate the beginning of a book by using the Bible's table of contents. Follow the numerical chapter numbers; these are usually in large type. Verses are likewise numbered in order within each chapter. Simply run your finger down the page until you locate the verse number you're looking for.

- If your Bible contains maps (usually in the back), consult them when cities, mountains, or seas are mentioned in your reading.

4 BEFRIEND THE WRITTEN TEXT.

Read with a pen or pencil in hand and underline passages of interest. Look up unfamiliar words in a dictionary. Write notes in the margins when necessary. The Bible was written to be read and used, not worshiped.

5 PRACTICE READING FROM THE BIBLE OUT LOUD.

BIBLE STUFF

THE FIVE BIGGEST MISCONCEPTIONS ABOUT THE BIBLE

1 THE BIBLE WAS WRITTEN IN A SHORT PERIOD OF TIME.

Christians believe that God inspired the Bible writers, the first of whom may have been Moses. God inspired people to write down important histories, traditions, songs, wise sayings, poetry, and prophetic words. All told—from the first recordings of the stories in Genesis to the last decisions about Revelation—the entire Bible was formed over a period spanning anywhere from 800 to 1,400 years!

2 ONE PERSON WROTE THE BIBLE.

Unlike Islam's Koran, which was written by the prophet Muhammad, the books of the Bible claim the handiwork of many people. Much of Scripture does not identify the human hand that wrote it, so some parts of the Bible may have been written by women as well as men.

3 THE ENTIRE BIBLE SHOULD BE TAKEN LITERALLY.

While many parts of the Bible are meant as descriptions of actual historical events, other parts are intended as *illustrations of God's truth*, such as Song of Solomon, the book of Revelation, and Jesus' parable of the good Samaritan. So when Jesus says, "If your right eye causes you to sin, tear it out and throw it away" (Matthew 5:29), please do not take the saying literally!

4 PEOPLE IN BIBLE TIMES WERE UNENLIGHTENED.
During the 1,400 years it took to write the Bible, some of history's greatest thinkers lived and worked. Many of these philosophers, architects, mathematicians, orators, theologians, historians, doctors, military tacticians, inventors, engineers, poets, and playwrights are still quoted today and their works are still in use.

5 THE BIBLE IS A SINGLE BOOK.
The Bible is actually a collection of books, letters, and other writings—more like a library than a book. There are 39 books in the Hebrew scriptures, what Christians call the "Old" Testament, and 27 books (mostly letters) in the New Testament. There are seven books in the Apocrypha (books written between the Old and New Testaments), or "deuterocanonical" books.

Old Testament begins

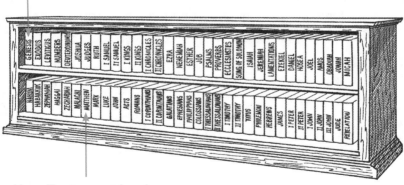

New Testament begins

The Bible is actually a library of many books all rolled up into one.

HOW TO MEMORIZE A BIBLE VERSE

Memorizing Scripture is an ancient faith practice. Its value is often mentioned by people who have, in crisis situations, remembered comforting or reassuring passages coming to mind, sometimes decades after first memorizing them. There are three common methods of memorization.

METHOD 1: MEMORIZE WITH MUSIC

Choose a verse that is special for you. It is more difficult to remember something that doesn't make sense to you or that lacks meaning.

1 **CHOOSE A FAMILIAR TUNE.**
Pick something catchy and repetitious.

2 **ADD THE WORDS FROM THE BIBLE VERSE TO YOUR TUNE.**
Mix up the words a bit, if necessary. Memorizing a verse "word for word" isn't always as important as learning the message of the verse.

3 **MARK THE VERSE IN YOUR BIBLE.**
This will help you find it again later on. Consider highlighting or underlining it.

4 **MAKE THE WORDS RHYME, IF POSSIBLE.**

METHOD 2: THE THREE S'S (SEE IT, SAY IT, SCRIPT IT)

This method works on the principle of multisensory reinforcement. The brain creates many more neural pathways to a memory through sight, speech, and manipulation (writing) than just one of these, so recall is quicker and easier.

1   WRITE THE VERSE ON INDEX CARDS IN LARGE PRINT. POST THE CARDS IN PLACES YOU REGULARLY LOOK, SUCH AS THE REFRIGERATOR DOOR OR BATHROOM MIRROR.

2   SAY THE VERSE OUT LOUD.
    Repeat the verse 10 times to yourself every time you notice one of your index cards.

3   WRITE THE VERSE DOWN.

4   TRY SAYING AND WRITING THE VERSE AT THE SAME TIME.
    Repeat.

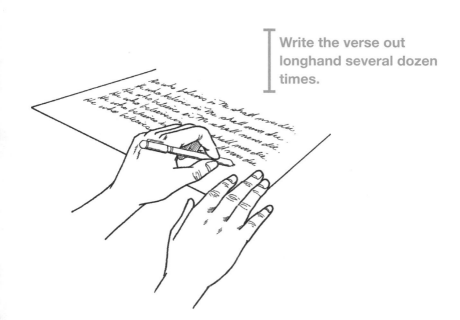

Write the verse out longhand several dozen times.

METHOD 3: OLD-FASHIONED MEMORIZATION

Attempt this method only if you consider yourself to be "old school" or if the other methods fail.

1 **WRITE THE VERSE OUT BY HAND ON PAPER.**
A whiteboard can work extremely well, also. Consider writing it as many as 100 times. Repeat this process until you can recite the verse flawlessly.

2 **DON'T GET UP UNTIL YOU'VE MEMORIZED THE VERSE.**
Open your Bible to the appropriate verse, sit down in front of it, and don't get up, eat, sleep, or use the bathroom until you can recite it flawlessly.

3 **ENLIST A FAMILY MEMBER OR FRIEND TO HELP YOU.**
Have them read along with you and prompt you when you get stuck.

THE TOP 10 BIBLE VILLAINS

1 SATAN

The Evil One is known by many names in the Bible and appears many places, but the devil's purpose is always the same: To disrupt and confuse people so they turn from God and seek to become their own gods. This Bible villain is still active today.

2 THE SERPENT

In Eden, the serpent succeeded in tempting Eve to eat from the tree of the knowledge of good and evil (Genesis 3:1-7). As a result, sin entered creation. If it weren't for the serpent, we'd all still be walking around naked, eating fresh fruit, and living forever.

3 PHARAOH (PROBABLY SETI I OR RAMESES II)

The notorious Pharaoh from the book of Exodus enslaved the Israelites. Moses eventually begged him to "Let my people go," but Pharaoh hardened his heart and refused. Ten nasty plagues later, Pharaoh relented, but then changed his mind again. In the end, with his army at the bottom of the sea, Pharaoh finally gave his slaves up to the wilderness.

4 GOLIATH

"The Philistine of Gath," who stood six cubits in height (about nine feet tall), was sent to fight David, still a downy-headed youth of 15. Goliath was a fighting champion known for killing people, but David drilled Goliath in the head with a rock from his sling and gave God the glory (1 Samuel 17).

BIBLE STUFF

one cubit

Though physically powerful, Goliath lost his battle with young David, one of the Top 10 heroes of the Bible.

Goliath   David

5 JEZEBEL

King Ahab of Judah's wife and a follower of the false god Baal, Jezebel led her husband away from God and tried to kill off the prophets of the Lord. Elijah the prophet, however, was on the scene. He shamed Jezebel's false prophets and killed them (1 Kings 18:40).

6 KING HEROD

Afraid of any potential threat to his power, upon hearing about the birth of the Messiah in Bethlehem Herod sent the Wise Men to pinpoint his location. Awestruck by the Savior in the cradle, the Wise Men went home by a different route and avoided Herod. In a rage, he ordered the murder of every child two years of age or younger in the vicinity of Bethlehem. The baby Messiah escaped with his parents to Egypt (Matthew 2:14-15).

7 THE PHARISEES, SADDUCEES, AND SCRIBES

They dogged Jesus throughout his ministry, alternately challenging his authority and being awed by his power. It was their leadership, with the consent and blessing of the people and the Roman government that brought Jesus to trial and execution.

8 JUDAS

One of Jesus' original disciples, Judas earned 30 pieces of silver by betraying his Lord over to the authorities. He accomplished this by leading the soldiers into the garden of Gethsemane where he revealed Jesus with a kiss (Matthew 26–27).

9 PONTIUS PILATE

The consummate politician, the Roman governor chose to preserve his own bloated status by giving the people what they wanted: Jesus' crucifixion. He washed his hands to signify self-absolution, but bloodied them instead.

10 GOD'S PEOPLE

They whine, they sin, they turn their backs on God over and over again. When given freedom, they blow it. When preached repentance by God's prophets, they stone them. When offered a Savior, we kill him. In the end, it must be admitted, God's people—us!—don't really shine. Only by God's grace and the gift of faith in Jesus Christ do we have hope.

THE TOP 10 BIBLE HEROES

The Bible is filled with typical examples of heroism, but another kind of hero inhabits the pages of the Bible—those people who, against all odds, follow God no matter the outcome. These are heroes of faith.

1 NOAH

In the face of ridicule from others, Noah trusted God when God chose him to build an ark to save a remnant of humanity from destruction. Noah's trust became part of a covenant with God.

Noah trusted God, even though others made fun of him. By following God's instructions and building a great ark, Noah and his family survived the flood (Genesis 6–10)

2 ABRAHAM AND SARAH

In extreme old age, Abraham and Sarah answered God's call to leave their home and travel to a strange land, where they became the parents of God's people.

3 MOSES

Moses, a man with a speech impediment, challenged the Egyptian powers to deliver God's people from bondage. He led a rebellious and contrary people for 40 years through the wilderness and gave them God's law.

4 RAHAB

A prostitute who helped Israel conquer the promised land, Rahab was the great-grandmother of King David, and thus a part of the family of Jesus himself.

5 DAVID

Great King David, the youngest and smallest member of his family, defeated great enemies, turning Israel into a world power. He wrote psalms, led armies, and confessed his sins to the Lord.

6 MARY AND JOSEPH

These humble peasants responded to God's call to be the parents of the Messiah, although the call came through a pregnancy that was not the result of marriage.

7 THE CANAANITE WOMAN

Desperate for her daughter's health, the Canaanite woman challenged Jesus regarding women and race by claiming God's love for all people (Matthew 15:21-28). Because of this, Jesus praised her faith.

BIBLE STUFF

8 PETER

Peter was a man quick to speak but slow to think. At Jesus' trial, Peter denied ever having known him. But in the power of forgiveness and through Christ's appointment, Peter became a leader in the early church.

9 SAUL/PAUL

Originally an enemy and persecutor of Christians, Paul experienced a powerful vision of Jesus, converted, and became the greatest missionary the church has ever known.

10 PHOEBE

A contemporary of Paul's, Phoebe is believed to have delivered the book of Romans after traveling some 800 miles from Cenchrea near Corinth to Rome. A wealthy woman, she used her influence to travel, protect other believers, and to host worship services in her home.

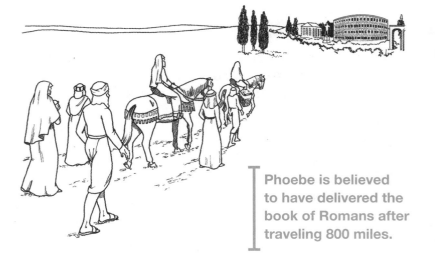

Phoebe is believed to have delivered the book of Romans after traveling 800 miles.

THE THREE MOST REBELLIOUS THINGS JESUS DID

1 THE PROPHET RETURNED TO HIS HOMETOWN (LUKE 4:14-27).
Jesus returned to Nazareth, where he was raised and was invited to read Scripture and preach. First, he insisted that the scriptures he read were not just comforting promises of a distant future, but that they were about him, local boy, anointed by God. Second, he insisted God would bless foreigners with those same promises through him. These statements amounted to the unpardonable crime of blasphemy!

2 THE REBEL THUMBED HIS NOSE AT THE AUTHORITIES (JOHN 11:55—12:11).
Jesus had become an outlaw, hunted by the religious authorities who wanted to kill him. Mary, Martha, and Lazarus threw a thank-you party for Jesus in Bethany, right outside Jerusalem, the authorities' stronghold. In spite of the threats to his life, Jesus went to the party. This was not just rebellion but a demonstration of how much Jesus loved his friends.

3 THE KING RODE A ROYAL PROCESSION RIGHT UNDER CAESAR'S NOSE (MATTHEW 21:1-17; MARK 11:1-10; LUKE 19:28-38; JOHN 12:12-19).
Jesus entered Jerusalem during a great festival, in full view of adoring crowds, as a king come home to rule. Riding the colt, heralded by the people with cloaks and branches, accompanied by the royal anthem (Psalm 118), he rode in to claim Jerusalem for God and himself as God's anointed. The Roman overlords and the Jewish leaders watched this seditious act and prepared for a crucifixion.

BIBLE STUFF

THE SEVEN FUNNIEST BIBLE STORIES

Humor isn't scarce in the Bible; you just have to look for it. For example, God tells Abraham (100 years old) and Sarah (in her 90s) they'll soon have a son. Understandably, they laugh. Later, they have a son named Isaac, which means "he laughs." Bible humor is also ironic, gross, and sometimes just plain bizarre.

1 GIDEON'S DOG-MEN (JUDGES 6:11—7:23)

God chooses Gideon to lead an army against the Midianites. Gideon gathers an army of 32,000 men, but this is too many. God tells Gideon to make all the men drink from a stream, and then selects only the 300 men who lap water like dogs.

2 DAVID AMBUSHES SAUL IN A CAVE WHILE HE'S "BUSY" (1 SAMUEL 24:2-7).

While pursuing David cross-country to engage him in battle, Saul goes into a cave to "relieve himself" (move his bowels). Unbeknownst to Saul, David and his men are already hiding in the very same cave. While Saul's doing his business, David sneaks up and cuts off a corner of Saul's cloak with a knife. Outside afterward, David shows King Saul the piece of cloth to prove he could have killed him "on the throne."

3 KING DAVID DOES THE GOOFY (2 SAMUEL 12-23).

David is so excited about bringing the Ark of the Covenant to Jerusalem that he dances before God and all the people dressed only in a linen ephod, an apron-like garment that covered only the front of his body.

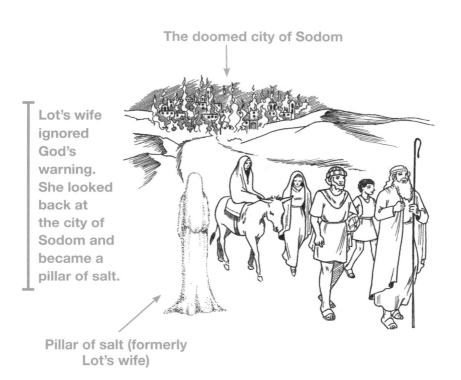

The doomed city of Sodom

Lot's wife ignored God's warning. She looked back at the city of Sodom and became a pillar of salt.

Pillar of salt (formerly Lot's wife)

4 LOT'S WIFE (GENESIS 19:24-26)
While fleeing God's wrath upon the cities of Sodom and Gomorrah, Lot's wife forgets (or ignores) God's warning not to look back upon the destruction and turns into a woman-sized pillar of salt.

5 GERASENE DEMONIAC (MARK 5:1-20)
A man is possessed by so many demons that chains cannot hold him. Jesus exorcises the demons and sends them into a herd of 2,000 pigs, which then run over the edge of a cliff and drown in the sea. The herders, now 2,000 pigs poorer, get miffed and ask Jesus to leave.

6 DISCIPLES AND LOAVES OF BREAD (MARK 8:14-21)

The disciples were there when Jesus fed 5,000 people with just five loaves of bread and two fish. They also saw him feed 4,000 people with seven loaves. Later, in a boat, the disciples fret to an exasperated Jesus because they have only one loaf for 13 people.

7 PETER CAN'T SWIM (MATTHEW 14:22-33).

Blundering Peter sees Jesus walking on the water and wants to join him. But when the wind picks up, Peter panics and starts to sink. In Greek, the name Peter means "rock."

Peter, "the rock," sank when he looked to himself instead of to Jesus. Jesus later described Peter as a Rock of the church (Matthew 16:18).

THE FIVE GROSSEST BIBLE STORIES

1 EGLON AND EHUD (JUDGES 3:12-30)
Before kings reigned over Israel, judges ruled the people. At that time, a very overweight king named Eglon conquered Israel and demanded money. A man named Ehud brought the payment to Eglon while he was perched on his "throne" (meaning "toilet"). Along with the money, Ehud handed over a little something extra—his sword, which he buried so far in Eglon's belly that the sword disappeared into the king's fat and, as the Bible says, "the dirt came out" (v. 22).

2 JOB'S SORES (JOB 2:1-10)
Job lived a righteous life yet he suffered anyway. He had oozing sores from the bald spot on top of his head clear down to the soft spot on the bottom of his foot. Job used a broken piece of pottery to scrape away the pus that leaked from his sores.

3 THE NAKED PROPHET (ISAIAH 20)
God's prophets went to great lengths to get God's message across to the people. Isaiah was no exception. God's people planned a war, but God gave it the thumbs down. Isaiah marched around Jerusalem naked *for three years* as a sign of what would happen if the people went to war.

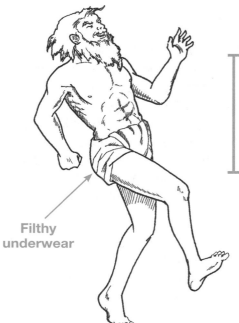

Jeremiah strapped on some filthy underwear to show God could no longer be proud of the people.

Filthy underwear

4 THE ALMOST-NAKED PROPHET (JEREMIAH 13:1-11)

God sent Jeremiah to announce that God could no longer be proud of the people. To make the point, Jeremiah bought a new pair of underwear, wore them every day without washing them, then buried them in the wet river sand. Later, he dug them up, strapped them on, and shouted that this is what has happened to the people who were God's pride!

5 SPILLING YOUR GUTS (MATTHEW 27:1-8; ACTS 1:16-19)

Judas betrayed Jesus and sold him out for 30 pieces of silver. He bought a field with the ill-gotten loot. Guilt-stricken, Judas walked out to the field, his belly swelled up until it burst, and his intestines spilled out on to the ground.

FIVE FACTS ABOUT LIFE IN OLD TESTAMENT TIMES

1 ALMOST EVERYONE WORE SANDALS.
They were called "sandals" because people walked on sand much of the time.

2 THERE WERE NO NEWSPAPERS.
People got news by hearing it from other people. Spreading important news was like a giant game of "telephone."

3 IT WAS DARK.
Homes, often tents, were typically lit at night by an oil lamp, if at all.

4 YOU HAD TO FETCH YOUR WATER, WHICH WAS SCARCE.
Rich folks had servants to carry it for them, but most people had to carry household water in jugs or leather bags, usually some distance, from a river or well.

5 LIFE EXPECTANCY WAS SHORT.
Despite some long-lived exceptions described in the book of Genesis, such as Abraham (175 years) and Methuselah (969 years), few people lived past 50.

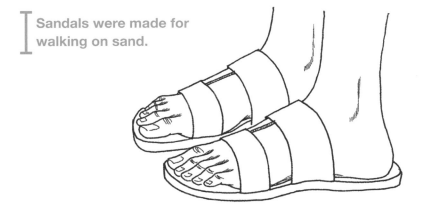

Sandals were made for walking on sand.

BIBLE STUFF

TEN IMPORTANT THINGS THAT HAPPENED BETWEEN THE OLD AND NEW TESTAMENTS

The period of time described in the Old Testament ended about 400 years before Jesus' birth. The people of God kept living, believing, struggling, and writing during that period. Here are some of the important events that took place between the Testaments.

1 THE HEBREW NATION DISSOLVED.
In 587 B.C.E., the Babylonians destroyed Jerusalem and Solomon's temple, and took the people into exile. Judah was never again an independent kingdom.

2 THE PEOPLE SCATTERED.
After the exile to Babylon ended, the people of Judah moved to many different places. Some of them later came back, but many never did. Some of them lived in Babylon, some lived in Egypt, and some just scattered elsewhere.

3 A RELIGION REPLACED A NATION.
As a result of items 1 and 2, the people's religion changed. They no longer had a state or national religion (Judean religion). Instead, they had a freestanding faith called Judaism.

4 THE ARAMAIC LANGUAGE BECAME POPULAR.
Because Aramaic was the international language of the Persian Empire, many Jews quit speaking Hebrew and spoke Aramaic instead. This is why Jesus spoke Aramaic.

5 ALEXANDER THE GREAT CONQUERED THE WORLD.
Around 330 B.C.E., Alexander the Great conquered the Mediterranean and Mesopotamian world. As a result, Greek became the everyday language of business and trade in the region. This is why the New Testament was written in Greek.

6 THE HAMMER DROPPED.
Around 170 B.C.E., the Seleucid emperor outlawed circumcision and the Sabbath, and defiled the temple. A family of Jews called the Maccabees (which means "hammer") led a revolt.

7 THE HEBREW SCRIPTURES WERE FINISHED.
During this time, the individual books that make up what we call the Old Testament were finished. Several other religious books written at this time (mostly in Greek) aren't in the Protestant Bible but are part of the Apocrypha.

8 THE SADDUCEES, PHARISEES, ESSENES, SAMARITANS, ZEALOTS, AND OTHER GROUPS OF PEOPLE SPROUTED UP.
Different schools of thought developed within Judaism. Most of their disagreements were over the idea that God's people would be resurrected to eternal life.

9 GOD SEEMED TO HAVE FORGOTTEN THE PROMISE.

God promised King David that one of his descendants would always be king in Jerusalem. But after the Babylonian exile, there were no kings in Jerusalem. People wondered what had happened to God's promise.

10 THE ROMAN EMPIRE EXPANDED.

In 63 B.C.E., the Roman Empire conquered Palestine, having already conquered pretty much everyone else in the region. This is why the Roman Empire ruled the area during the time of Jesus and the New Testament.

FIVE FACTS ABOUT LIFE
IN NEW TESTAMENT TIMES

1 SYNAGOGUES WERE NOT ALWAYS BUILDINGS.
For worship, Jesus' people gathered in all kinds of places,
often outdoors. "Church" was any gathering of people for
worship.

2 HOUSES WERE BOXY.
Most houses had a flat roof with an outside staircase leading
to it. Inhabitants would sleep on the roof during hot weather.

Houses in New Testament times
were boxy.

3   **EVERY TOWN HAD A MARKETPLACE.**
Usually there was just one marketplace per town, but one
could buy almost everything needed to live.

4   **PEOPLE ATE A LOT OF FISH.**
The most common fish in the Sea of Galilee were catfish and
carp. Roasting over a charcoal fire was the most common
method of cooking.

5   **DOGS WERE SHUNNED.**
The Jewish people in Jesus' day did not keep dogs as pets.
Dogs were considered unclean because they ate garbage and
animal carcasses.

JESUS' TWELVE APOSTLES (PLUS JUDAS AND PAUL)

While Jesus had many disciples (students and followers) the Bible focuses particularly on twelve who were closest to him. Tradition says that these twelve spread Jesus' message throughout the known world (Matthew 28:18-20). For this reason, they were known as *apostles*, a word that means "sent ones."

1 **ANDREW**

A fisherman and the first disciple to follow Jesus, Andrew brought his brother, Simon Peter, to Jesus.

2 **BARTHOLOMEW**

Also called Nathanael, tradition has it that he was martyred by being skinned alive.

3 **JAMES THE ELDER**

James, with John and Peter, was one of Jesus' closest disciples. Herod Agrippa killed James because of his faith, which made him a martyr (Acts 12:2).

4 **JOHN**

John (or one of his followers) is thought to be the author of the Gospel of John and three letters of John. He probably died of natural causes in old age.

5 **MATTHEW**

Matthew was a tax collector and, therefore, probably an outcast even among his own people. He is attributed with the authorship of the Gospel of Matthew.

6 PETER

Peter was a fisherman who was brought to faith by his brother Andrew. He was probably martyred in Rome by being crucified upside down.

7 PHILIP

Philip, possibly a Greek, is responsible for bringing Bartholomew (Nathanael) to faith. He is thought to have died in a city called Phrygia.

8 JAMES THE LESS

James was called "the Less" so he wouldn't be confused with James, the brother of John, or James, Jesus' brother.

9 SIMON

Simon is often called "the Zealot." Zealots were a political group in Jesus' day that favored the overthrow of the Roman government by force.

10 JUDE

Jude may have worked with Simon the Zealot in Persia (Iran) where they were martyred on the same day.

11 THOMAS

"Doubting" Thomas preached the message of Jesus in India.

12 MATTHIAS

Matthias was chosen by lot to replace Judas. It is thought that he worked mostly in Ethiopia.

13 JUDAS ISCARIOT

Judas was the treasurer for Jesus' disciples and the one who betrayed Jesus for 30 pieces of silver. According to the Bible, Judas killed himself for his betrayal.

14 PAUL

Paul is considered primarily responsible for bringing non-Jewish people to faith in Jesus. He traveled extensively and wrote many letters to believers. Many of Paul's letters are included in the New Testament.

THE FIVE WEIRDEST LAWS IN THE OLD TESTAMENT

The Old Testament has many helpful, common sense laws, such as "You shall not kill," and, "You shall not steal." But there are a few others that need some explaining.

1 THE "OX" LAW

"When an ox gores a man or a woman to death, the ox shall be stoned, and its flesh shall not be eaten; but the owner of the ox shall not be liable" (Exodus 21:28). Replace "ox" with "car" and the law makes more sense—it is about protecting others from reckless actions.

People living in biblical times were sometimes gored by oxen.

People who were gored by oxen—or victims of other crimes—had legal recourse.

2 THE "NO KID BOILING" LAW

"You shall not boil a kid in its mother's milk" (Exodus 23:19b). A "kid," of course, is a juvenile goat, not a human being.

3 THE "WHICH BUGS ARE LEGAL TO EAT" LAW

"All winged insects that walk upon all fours are detestable to you. But among the winged insects that walk on all fours you may eat those that have jointed legs above their feet" (Leviticus 11:20-21). The law is unclear whether it is legal to eat the bug if you first pull off the legs.

4 THE "DON'T EAT BLOOD" LAW

"No person among you shall eat blood" (Leviticus 17:12). Some laws beg the question whether people in that time had any sense of taste.

5 THE "PURE CLOTH" LAW

"You shall not wear clothes made of wool and linen woven together" (Deuteronomy 22:11). Polyester came along after Bible times, but certainly blends are legal.

BIBLE STUFF

THE TOP 10 BIBLE MIRACLES AND WHAT THEY MEAN

1 CREATION

God created the universe and everything that is in it, and God continues to create and recreate without ceasing. God's first and ongoing miracle was to reveal that the creation has a purpose.

2 THE PASSOVER

The Israelites were enslaved by Pharaoh, a ruler who believed the people belonged to him, not to God. In the last of 10 plagues, God visited the houses of all the Egyptians to kill the firstborn male in each one. God alone is Lord of the people, and no human can claim ultimate power over us.

3 THE EXODUS

God's people were fleeing Egypt when Pharaoh dispatched his army to force them back into slavery. The army trapped the people with their backs to a sea, but God parted the water and the people walked across to freedom while Pharaoh's minions were destroyed. God chose to free us from all forms of tyranny so we may use that freedom to serve God and each other.

4 MANNA

After the people crossed the sea to freedom, they complained that they were going to starve to death. They even asked to go back to Egypt. God sent manna, a form of bread, so the people lived. God cares for us even when we give up, pine for our slavery, and lose faith. God never abandons us.

5 THE INCARNATION

The immortal and infinite God became a human being, choosing to be born of a woman. God loved us enough to become one of us in Jesus of Nazareth, forever bridging the divide that had separated us from God.

6 JESUS HEALED THE PARALYZED MAN.

Some men brought a paralyzed friend to Jesus. Jesus said, "Son, your sins are forgiven" (Mark 2:5). This means that Jesus has the power to forgive our sins—and he does so as a free gift.

7 JESUS CALMED THE STORM.

Jesus was asleep in a boat with his disciples when a great storm came up and threatened to sink it. He said, "Peace! Be still!" (Mark 4:39). Then the storm immediately calmed. Jesus is Lord over even the powers of nature.

8 THE RESURRECTION

Human beings executed Jesus, but God raised him from the dead on the third day. Through baptism, we share in Jesus' death, so we will also share in eternal life with God the Father, Son, and Holy Spirit. Christ conquered death.

9 PENTECOST

Jesus ascended from the earth, but he did not leave the church powerless or alone. On the 50th day after the Jewish Passover (*Pentecost* means 50th), Jesus sent the Holy Spirit to create the church and take up residence among us. The Holy Spirit is present with us always.

10 THE SECOND COMING

One day, Christ will come again and end all suffering. This means that the final result of the epic battle between good and evil is already assured. It is simply that evil has not yet admitted defeat.

BIBLE STUFF

TOP FIVE SCARY MONSTERS IN THE BIBLE

1 THE RED DRAGON (REVELATION 12)

This serpentine creature has seven heads with a crown on each, plus 10 horns. This dragon not only opposes God but also ultimately reveals itself as the devil.

Monsters in the Bible are often described as quite scary. The red dragon in Revelation 12 is one of the scarier ones. Lutherans tend to look somewhat askance at monsters.

2 THE BEAST FROM THE SEA (REVELATION 13)

Not to be confused with the red dragon or Leviathan, this otherworldly fiend gains all his power from the dragon and makes others swear allegiance to him. He bears the unlikely combination of a leopard's body, a bear's feet, and a lion's mouth. His seven heads each bear blasphemous names, along with 10 horns and 10 crowns.

Somewhat less terrifying, but still pretty scary, is the satyr, mentioned in Isaiah 13:21.

3 RAHAB (ISAIAH 51)

A mythical sea monster from Babylonian legend, she represents chaos and destruction—not to mention the pagan faith opposing the Israelites. (The Rahab from Isaiah 51 should not be confused with the woman mentioned in Joshua 2:1-21; 6:17-25; and Matthew 1:5.)

4 LEVIATHAN (JOB 3)

Since the sea represented the chaotic unknown to the Israelites, anything living in it scared them. Even though Leviathan was likely just a whale, the very fact that it lived in the abyss made it creepy.

5 SATYRS OR GOAT-DEMONS (ISAIAH 13:21)

A satyr, also popular in Greek mythology, is a man with goat legs, ears, and horns. Popular images of Satan are often derived from this creature.

TOP SEVEN DASTARDLY BIBLE DEEDS

The Bible is adult literature. It is about real life and does not sugarcoat it. The Bible includes countless tales of murder, theft, sexual assault, and of people breaking every commandment in graphic detail.

1 **ADAM AND EVE SIN (GENESIS 3).**
   Eve and Adam ate the forbidden fruit: the first sin. Adam blamed it on his wife. The earth was cursed because of their sin.

Perhaps the most dastardly deed in the Bible is Adam and Eve's original sin, the one that started it all.

BIBLE STUFF

2 CAIN KILLS ABEL (GENESIS 4).

Brothers Cain and Abel both offered God gifts. Cain offered God's gifts from the cursed earth, so God liked Abel's gift better. In a jealous fit, Cain killed Abel, but God had mercy on Cain and did not kill him in return.

3 PHAROAH'S TYRANNY (EXODUS 1–15)

Pharaoh grew afraid of the Israelites in his country, so he enslaved them. When they grew too numerous, he ordered that all newborn boys be killed. Even after he agreed to let the people go, Pharaoh changed his mind and pursued the people with his army.

4 DAVID TAKES BATHSHEBA, KILLS URIAH (2 SAMUEL 11).

King David's personal life included more dastardly deeds than any television miniseries ever dreamed up. David forced sex on Bathsheba, Uriah's wife, and then sent Uriah to a certain death in battle to cover it up.

5 HEROD SLAUGHTERS THE INNOCENTS (MATTHEW 2:1-18).

When the Wise Men told King Herod that they had come to worship the child who had been born as the new King of the Jews, Herod tried to trick the Wise Men into leading him to the child. When that failed, he ordered that all boys under two years of age be killed.

6 JESUS' CRUCIFIXION (MARK 14–15)

Crucifixion was an exceptionally dastardly way of torturing a person to death. The victim did not bleed to death, but slowly died from asphyxiation due to the weight of his or her own body. The Roman governor Pilate and other authorities knew Jesus was innocent, but allowed the people to crucify him anyway.

7 SAUL PERSECUTES THE CHURCH (ACTS 1–9).

Saul of Tarsus persecuted the church, trying to stomp out those who followed Jesus. But as Paul, he repented and became a follower of Jesus himself. God's mercy is wide enough to forgive any dastardly deed.

TOP SEVEN ACTS OF HUMAN KINDNESS IN THE BIBLE

For all its shocking violence, the acts of mercy and kindness described in the Bible are perhaps even more shocking. The scandalous thing is that the people who offer kindness are often the people we would least expect to do so.

1 ESAU, THE BETTER BROTHER? (GENESIS 32)

Jacob stole Esau's birthright. Decades later, Esau goes to meet Jacob with 400 armed men. Remembering Esau's vow to kill him, Jacob is terrified. But Esau runs to meet him with heartfelt tears and generous gifts.

2 JOSEPH PITIES HIS BROTHERS (GENESIS 50).

Joseph's brothers threw him in a pit and sold him into slavery. Years later, when he could make them pay, he repays them with gifts and the offer of a new life with him in Egypt.

3 PHARAOH'S DAUGHTER PULLS MOSES FROM THE REEDS (EXODUS 2).

Pharaoh's daughter saves Moses from a soggy death and adopts him as her own son. The pagan princess holds the power of life and changes everything for God's people.

4 NAOMI ADOPTS RUTH (RUTH 1).

After the death of both of their husbands, daughter-in-law Ruth chooses to remain with Naomi and share her life and faith, rather than return to her own home. Here devotion, hope, and love become one.

Acts of kindness in the Bible are usually committed by unlikely persons. In this case, Pharaoh's daughter adopts Moses, a Hebrew baby, as her own son, saving him from certain death.

5   **JOB'S FRIENDS GRIEVE WITH HIM (JOB 2:11-13).**
Job has lost everything. His friends Eliphaz, Bildad, and
Zophar hear of his suffering and go to comfort him. They sit
with Job for seven days and nights. Good counselors, they do
not speak but simply share his grief. They only mess up later
when they start to talk.

6   **STEPHEN FORGIVES HIS EXECUTIONERS (ACTS
7:54-60).**
Stephen, one of the seven chosen to administer help to wid-
ows, is stoned to death because of his powerfully irritating
public witness to Christ. As he is dying he asks God to forgive
those who kill him.

7   **THE SINFUL WOMAN WASHES JESUS' FEET
(LUKE 7:36-50).**
A woman known only as a "sinner" dares to enter a Pharisee's
home where Jesus is dining. She washes Jesus' feet with her
tears, dries them with her hair, and anoints his feet with oint-
ment that costs a fortune.

TOP FIVE SIBLING RIVALRIES IN THE BIBLE

Fights between brothers and sisters are far from a new phenomenon. In fact, one might consider all such conflicts biblical.

1 CAIN AND ABEL (GENESIS 4)
Abel was a shepherd and Cain a farmer. When God favors the "keeper of sheep" (Abel) over the "tiller of the ground" (Cain), Cain invites Abel to a field to murder his younger brother. Here begins the history of sibling squabbles—not a great precedent.

2 JACOB AND ESAU (GENESIS 27)
Issac and Rebekah had two grown sons, Esau and Jacob—twins born only minutes apart. While Esau, a hairy man, was out hunting game in anticipation of his birthright, younger brother Jacob and their own mother schemed to deceive Isaac in his old age so that Jacob might receive the birthright intended for Esau. What can you expect from two who struggled even in their mother's womb?

3 JOSEPH AND HIS BROTHERS (GENESIS 37–46)
When Joseph, the beloved son of Jacob, shared his dream of greatness with his brothers, they had had enough. They sold him to the Ishmaelites, dipped his robe in goat's blood, and tricked their distraught father into believing he had been killed. Despite this conspiracy, Jacob *does* rise to greatness in Egypt and eventually saves his family from famine.

BIBLE STUFF

4 SOLOMON AND ADONIJAH (1 KINGS 1–2)

As King David grew old, it came time for him to name his successor. His son Adonijah declared himself king. But Bathsheba and the prophet Nathan worked to put Bathsheba's son, Solomon, on the throne. When Adonijah requested one of Solomon's concubines for a wife, Solomon took the request as a threat. Solomon had Adonijah killed and eventually became king.

5 MARY AND MARTHA (LUKE 10)

When Jesus visited the house of the sisters Mary and Martha, Martha went to great lengths to make preparations for the guest. When Mary sat at Jesus' feet rather than doing her chores, Martha complained to Jesus for Mary's lack of help.

Martha

Mary   Jesus

Siblings have always had a predisposition to be at odds with each other, even in the Bible. One of the most famous rivalries was between the industrious Martha and her attentive sister, Mary, when Jesus came to visit.

HOW TO IDENTIFY AN ANGEL

The word *angel* means "messenger" in both the Hebrew of the Old Testament and the Greek of the New Testament. In the Bible, God uses angels to communicate with people—to advise, call, protect, warn, judge, kill, bless, instruct, comfort, make birth announcements, and bring good news to them. When an angel shows up, somebody is in for an awe-inspiring, bone-rattling, life-changing experience. Here's how to be sure you're dealing with the real thing.

1 **TRY TO DETERMINE WHETHER GOD MIGHT SEND AN ANGEL IN THOSE SPECIFIC CIRCUMSTANCES OR WHETHER YOU MIGHT BE IMAGINING THINGS.**
Finding a lost wallet and someone opening a door for you when you have your arms full probably don't qualify as angelic encounters. Be careful not to diminish an angel's work in your life by confusing it with made-up encounters or attributing everyday coincidences or kindnesses to an angel.

2 **LISTEN FOR A GODLY MESSAGE.**
In the Bible, God almost never sends an angel without sending a message. Keep in mind that God's messages sometimes include judgment and wrath as well as comfort, grace, and healing. Look also for prophecies of impending future events.

3 **DISCERN WHICH TYPE OF ANGEL YOU MIGHT BE DEALING WITH.**
   - *Old Testament angels:* Encounters with these angels are sometimes bizarre and even hazardous, but also occasionally playful. You might get your hip knocked out of its socket (Genesis 32:25) or your foot crushed (Numbers 22:25), but you might also receive good culinary advice (Judges 6:20) or protection from hungry lions (Daniel 6:22).

- **New Testament angels:** These messengers appear chiefly to deliver good news and don't seem to get too involved in matters physically, though they reserve the right to do so when necessary (Matthew 28:2; John 5:4).

- **Modern-day angels:** These angels seem to bring primarily feelings of happiness, protection, and preservation, though very seldom a message. The discrepancy with the biblical models has caused some to question the authenticity of some modern-day encounters.

4 TAKE TIME TO GRAPPLE WITH YOUR ANGELIC ENCOUNTER BEFORE MAKING FINAL JUDGMENTS AND ANNOUNCING IT TO EVERYONE.

If it truly was an angelic encounter, God will make that clear over time, perhaps even sending the angel for repeat visits until you get the message. If not, blabbing about a questionable event might make you look like a kook.

BE AWARE

] Avoid confusing an angel with God. Angels sometimes appear subtly and slip into roles the Bible attributes only to God. Angels cannot deliver salvation, grace, or forgiveness of sins.

] Hunches, intuition, and a "sixth sense" are not signs of an angelic message from God. If an angel brings a message, you'll know it.

] Angels are not believed to use telepathy, coincidence, or other cryptic signals to communicate, as in some modern-day reports. God-sent angels typically speak their messages out loud.

HOW TO IDENTIFY AN ANGEL

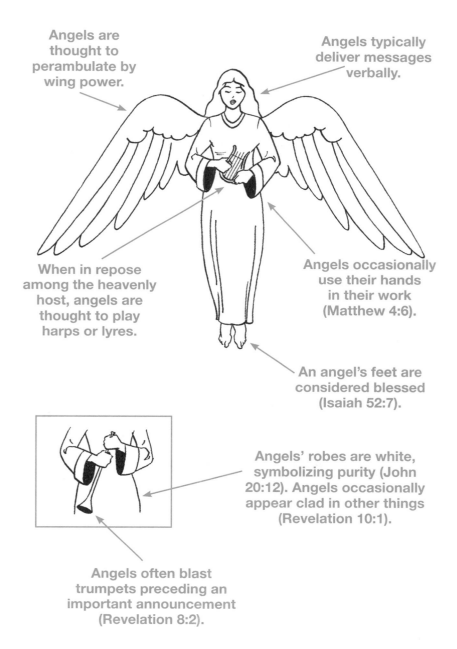

Angels are thought to perambulate by wing power.

Angels typically deliver messages verbally.

When in repose among the heavenly host, angels are thought to play harps or lyres.

Angels occasionally use their hands in their work (Matthew 4:6).

An angel's feet are considered blessed (Isaiah 52:7).

Angels' robes are white, symbolizing purity (John 20:12). Angels occasionally appear clad in other things (Revelation 10:1).

Angels often blast trumpets preceding an important announcement (Revelation 8:2).

BIBLE STUFF

TOP 10 ANGEL SIGHTINGS IN THE BIBLE

The term *angel* actually comes from the Greek word for "messenger." Here are 10 of the approximately 275 places in the Bible where God's special messengers are mentioned.

1 BALAAM AND HIS DONKEY (NUMBERS 22:22-35)
Becoming angry at his donkey, Balaam struck it three times, after which they have a heated exchange (yes, a talking donkey). An angel shows up to see what Balaam's up to.

Angels, God's messengers, do not always appear clothed in radiant garments and singing hymns. The three that visited Abraham and Sarah as they tented near the oaks of Mamre were mysterious and indistinct, and their message was quite strange.

2 THE ANNUNCIATION (LUKE 1:26-38)

God sent the angel Gabriel to Mary, a young teenager, to tell her she would bear a child who "will be called Son of the Most High." And so began Mary's life as the earthly mother of Jesus.

3 JOSEPH CONSIDERS DIVORCE (MATTHEW 1:18-25).

On learning the news of Mary's pregnancy, her fiancé Joseph was determined to break off their relationship. But an angel appeared to Joseph in a dream to explain that Mary had conceived a child by the Holy Spirit and would bear the savior of the world.

4 THE SHEPHERDS IN THE FIELDS (LUKE 2:8-15)

Perhaps one of the most famous angel stories, several appeared to the shepherds to announce the news of Jesus' birth: "Glory to God in the highest heaven, and on earth peace among those whom he favors!"

5 ABRAHAM, SARAH, AND THE THREE STRANGERS (GENESIS 18:1-15)

When three strangers appeared at Abraham and Sarah's home, Abraham ordered his servants to lavish the guests with choice food and drink. Later they discover the visitors are God's messengers sent to inform Sarah, though an old woman, that she would bear a son.

6 THE ANGEL GUARDING EDEN (GENESIS 3:23-24)

After their fall from God's favor, Adam and Eve were ordered to leave the Garden of Eden. At the garden's entrance, God placed an angel with a twirling fiery sword to guard against their return.

BIBLE STUFF

7 THE EMPTY TOMB (LUKE 24:1-9)

When a group of women went to anoint Jesus' crucified body, they found the tomb empty. Two angels startled them, telling the women that Jesus had risen from the dead.

8 JOHN OF PATMOS AND THE ANGEL (REVELATION 1:1-2)

The Lord sent an angel to John to share with him God's plan for the end of time. The book of Revelation is what was "revealed" in his vision.

9 FEMALE ANGELS (ZECHARIAH 5:9)

Angels are spirits, not humans, though they sometimes have a human form when they appear on earth. Most of the Bible's angels are described with male characteristics, although Zechariah 5:9 gives the impression that two angels had female forms.

10 DANIEL'S FIERY ANGEL (DANIEL 10:5-6)

Not all angels are described as having human characteristics. Daniel sees an angel wearing an assortment of jewels with a face like lightning and eyes like torches.

FIVE MOST COMMON IMAGES FOR GOD IN THE BIBLE

Descriptions of God in the Bible are so many as to make a complete compilation too lengthy for this little book, as are the various names for God. But there are at least five images common enough to mention as standouts.

1 FATHER
God is depicted as the father of the nation Israel (Exodus 4:22-23) and Jesus calls God "Abba! Father" (Mark 14:36).

There are many vibrant and important images for God in the Bible, but Lutherans tend to prefer the Trinitarian Formula as a reliable name for God because we're not huge risk-takers.

2 CREATOR

God's act of creating the universe and everything in it (Genesis 1–2) is arguably God's defining characteristic (in many psalms). In other words, to be God is to be one who creates.

3 KING

God tried to talk Israel out of demanding a king, saying, "I am . . . your King" (Isaiah 43:15). God is called the power behind every throne (1 Samuel 16:13). Jesus turned the title on its head by making the cross his throne and wearing a crown of thorns.

4 JUDGE

In one of Jesus' clearest teachings about what God will do at the end of time, he says that God will judge people on the basis of how we have treated one another (Matthew 25:31-46).

5 MOTHER

Images of caregiving, nurturing, and loving that make us think of mothers are often used for God's interactions with human beings (Isaiah 66:12-13). Jesus uses the imagery of a mother hen (Luke 13:34) to describe his relationship to his people.

BE AWARE

] Because of the superabundance of distinct images and names for God in the Bible, many people avoid adhering to a single one for too long at a stretch, referring to God in many ways. Others stick with a single name or referent for God their whole lives.

] The Trinitarian Formula accepted by Lutherans, "Father, Son, and Holy Spirit," is most commonly used in worship and is often regarded as God's name.

] Regardless of the name you use to refer to God, the Second Commandment still applies.

TOP FIVE "OTHER GODS" IN THE OLD TESTAMENT AND WHO BELIEVED IN THEM

The Old Testament is filled with warnings to the Israelites—usually ignored—against worshiping "other gods."

1 BAAL HADAD (OCCURS FREQUENTLY IN THE OLD TESTAMENT)

The great Canaanite god of storm and fertility. Baal gave the Lord some serious competition among the Lord's people. Ahab, for example, built an altar for Baal in Samaria in Israel, and Manasseh did the same in Jerusalem. Baal Hadad is usually depicted holding lightning bolts in his hands, prepared to strike.

2 ASHERAH (JEREMIAH 7:17-18)

A Canaanite mother-goddess. Like the Canaanites, Hebrews erected and worshiped carved poles representing her. Some Israelites even believed she was God's companion. The prophets repeatedly condemned the worship of Asherah.

3 ASTARTE (JEREMIAH 7:16-20; 44:15-19)

Originally a Canaanite war-goddess worshiped by the Philistines (1 Samuel 31:10). Astarte was probably associated with the Jerusalem "Queen of Heaven" cult against which Jeremiah preached.

4 DAGON (1 SAMUEL 5:1-7)

The Philistines are said to have built temples for the warrior god Dagon, although none have yet been found. It is not known whether Dagon was a god related to a "fish man" or a god of grain.

BIBLE STUFF

5 MOLECH (1 KINGS 11:5, 33)

A Canaanite god of fire also worshiped in Assyria. Sacrifices to Molech involved passing children through fire. Solomon was condemned for building a high place to Molech. This god had a sanctuary just south of Jerusalem.

Molech, the Canaanite god of fire, is one of the lesser-known gods in the Bible and doesn't get much press. He is sometimes called "Milcom" in the Old Testament.

THE FIVE MOST UNPOPULAR OLD TESTAMENT PROPHETS

New Testament tax collectors weren't alone in being hated by God's people. Here are five notorious bearers of God's message and what made them so unpopular.

1 AMOS

Amos gained few friends when he told the Israelites that their privilege came with responsibility. He prophesied against Israel's enemies and then showed Israel's practices were actually worse than the nations they hated. He even said that Israel would be destroyed. Amos let God's people know that God hates violence and oppression of the weak—no matter who's doing it.

2 NAHUM

Nahum told God's people that even a mighty army wouldn't keep a nation safe from God's judgment. About 150 years earlier, Jonah had told the Ninevites to repent (and they did), but they quickly returned to old ways. God gave Nahum a new message of destruction for the Ninevites, but they weren't scared because they had a strong army. So while the city was falling, Nahum ridiculed them by suggesting they draw water (in the midst of a flood), and add bricks to the already demolished city wall.

3 MICAH

Micah told the people that God wants disciples to have humble hearts and behavior that is just and kind to others. He said God would come and destroy the nation of Judah because the powerful had schemed to steal from the poor and followed false prophets. They thought following ritual was enough. It wasn't.

BIBLE STUFF

4 ZEPHANIAH

Zephaniah was another prophet in Judah. He made his enemies by warning that even those who refused to worship idols would face God's judgment because they didn't follow God.

5 JEREMIAH

God called Jeremiah to be a prophet when he was just a boy. This gave him more time to confront God's people about their self-focused lives. He was persecuted bitterly by Judah's last two kings—and even his own extended family tried to kill him. Jeremiah's messages were many—but this one still speaks: Those who are godly may suffer persecution, but they should look to God for salvation!

The Lord's prophets tended to be unpopular, especially among the wealthy, because their messages called for justice toward others and fidelity toward God. Amos was particularly unpopular for this reason.

FIVE INSPIRING WOMEN IN THE BIBLE

There are more than 300 women mentioned in the Bible. Some have names, others are referred to as "the women" or some other similar designation. Theologians and scholars have begun to highlight the lives of these many women and speak of their contributions to the story of God. Here are a few of the more inspiring examples.

1 **MIRIAM, JOCHEBED, PUAH, SHIPHRAH, AND PHARAOH'S DAUGHTER**
These five women were instrumental in the survival of Moses. Without their quick thinking, strong courage, and love of God, Moses would have drowned in the Nile River along with many other baby boys. *Note: We are naming more than one woman in this instance, but that's fine. It's a single story that involves them all.*

2 **RUTH**
Ruth chose not to return to her homeland and family after the death of her husband in order to attend to the needs of her mother-in-law, Naomi. Ruth showed intelligence and compassion in gaining the security she and Naomi needed upon their return to Israel. Other women in the story even remarked that Ruth was more valuable than having a son—a high compliment in those days of male preference.

3 **ESTHER**
When an evil man threatened to annihilate her people, Queen Esther used her beauty and skills in negotiation to save them. Esther is commemorated each year during Purim, a Jewish holiday.

4 LYDIA

Lydia was known as a God fearer, a follower of God who regularly prayed with her household. She began a house church and attended to the needs of the apostle Paul. Her house may have been the first European Christian congregation.

5 MARY, THE MOTHER OF THE LORD

At a young age, Mary answered a resounding "YES" to the angel's request that she bear God's Son.

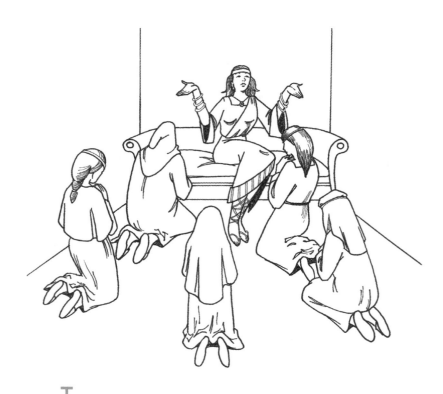

Lydia was a "God fearer," someone who received the gospel of Jesus Christ and was used to spread the good news in her town.

TOP FIVE MISCONCEPTIONS ABOUT THE BOOK OF REVELATION

The book of Revelation is among the most misunderstood—and misused—books in all written literature. In fact, some people make a good living misinterpreting Revelation for others with apocalyptic fiction. Lutherans, however, enjoy debunking these myths.

1 **THE AUTHOR OF REVELATION WAS JOHN, THE DISCIPLE OF JESUS, SON OF ZEBEDEE.**
   The writer's name was John (a common New Testament name), but not John the apostle. In chapter 21, he refers to "the twelve" with no hint that he was one of them.

2 **COMBINING REVELATION WITH OTHER BIBLICAL END-TIME REFERENCES REVEALS A HIDDEN SCHEDULE FOR CHRIST'S RETURN.**
   Many rapture theories take verses from Daniel, Matthew, 1 and 2 Thessalonians, and 1 John and combine them with parts of Revelation to construct their apocalyptic scenarios. This treats the Bible like a box of puzzle pieces. It's better to read Revelation on its own, as a whole book with integrity and unity.

3 **REVELATION IS ONLY ABOUT THE FUTURE.**
   Revelation is not a future history of the end of the world, or a mysterious, coded prediction that will only be understood later. It is a letter written to be read to first-century Christian churches. "John to the seven churches that are in Asia" (Revelation 1:4). Revelation's message would have been pretty clearly understood by its original hearers.

4 REVELATION IS ONLY ABOUT THE PAST.
Much of the letter is probably symbolic of imperial Rome. However, there is also much in it about God's future salvation for the world. Plus, what Revelation teaches about remaining faithful and hopeful in a faithless and challenging world speaks to all Christians today.

5 REVELATION IS JUST TOO WEIRD TO HEAR READ OUT LOUD IN WORSHIP.
On the contrary, much of our liturgy comes from Revelation, as well as the words of many favorite hymns, including "Holy, Holy, Holy," "Alabare," "Who Is This Host Arrayed in White," "For All the Saints," and "Shall We Gather at the River?"

BE AWARE

]   The book is not called "Revelations," with an "s," as many people incorrectly say, but Revelation. No "s" at the end, please.

]   The return of Christ cannot be ignored; it is a crucial part of our faith. When we say the Apostles' Creed we confess, "He will come again to judge the living and the dead."

Among the most common misconceptions about the book of Revelation is the idea that it is plural.

HOW TO TELL WHEN THE APOCALYPSE IS IMMINENT

There has been a great deal of best-selling speculation about the Apocalypse—Christ's Second Coming. Here's what to look for— or *not* look for, as the case may be—based on what Jesus said.

1 **IT'LL BE MOSTLY INVISIBLE TO THE NAKED EYE.**
   "The kingdom of God is not coming with things that can be observed," said Jesus (Luke 17:20). Don't rely on television coverage or newspaper headlines for signs.

2 **PEOPLE WILL SIMPLY GO ABOUT THEIR DAILY BUSINESS.**
   When the End is near, people will eat and drink, buy and sell, plant and build, marry, and so on (Luke 17:27-28). It will be "business as usual."

3 **SOME CHRISTIANS WILL BE IN FOR A ROUGH TIME.**
   Jesus' followers will suffer like he did, and will testify to their faith (Luke 21:12).

4 **IT WILL BE DIFFICULT TO DISTINGUISH IT FROM OTHER DAYS.**
   There will be wars, earthquakes, famines, plagues, and unrest in the Middle East (Luke 21:20-24).

5 **PROPHETS AND FALSE PROPHETS WILL RISE.**
   Some people will claim that they see signs of Jesus' coming (Luke 21:25-27).

BIBLE STUFF

BE AWARE

] When asked what he would do if he knew the world would end tomorrow, Martin Luther said he would plant a tree today. To expect Christ's coming is not to live in fear, but in the joyful expectation that "your redemption is drawing near" (Luke 21:28).

When asked what he would do if he knew the world would end tomorrow, Martin Luther said he would plant a tree today. To expect Christ's coming again is not to live in fear but in joyful expectation.

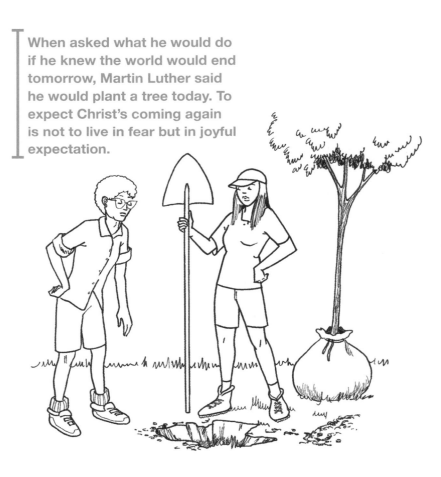

SEVEN IMPORTANT BIBLE TEACHINGS EVERY LUTHERAN SHOULD KNOW

The Lutheran tradition, which takes its name from a Bible teacher who did his job with profound thoroughness, has always centered its conversations and proclamations in the Bible. At minimum, a basic understanding of these passages can help keep you on track.

1 THE BIBLE IS THE WRITTEN AND INSPIRED WORD OF GOD (2 TIMOTHY 3:16).

The Bible records and announces God's redemption in Jesus and God's presence through the Holy Spirit (Hebrews 4:12). The Bible is the authoritative source and norm of the church's proclamation, faith, and life.

2 THERE IS ONE GOD (DEUTERONOMY 6:4).

Our one God exists in three persons: the Father, the Son, and the Holy Spirit (Matthew 3:16-17; 28:19). This One God existed before the beginning of the world (Genesis 1:1-3) and sent Jesus as our true way of salvation (John 3:16).

3 JESUS CHRIST IS LORD AND SAVIOR (COLOSSIANS 1:15-20).

Jesus was completely human and completely divine. He asks us to believe in our hearts and confess with our lips that he is our Lord and Savior (Romans 10:8-9). Jesus is God Incarnate, who offers us salvation by God's grace through faith for good works (Ephesians 2:8-10).

4 THE HOLY SPIRIT IS THE INDWELLING PRESENCE OF GOD (JOHN 20:22).

The Holy Spirit convicts us of sin (Romans 3:21-23) but also promises regeneration and salvation for all who believe (Romans 3:24-26). Lutherans believe that the Holy Spirit calls, gathers, enlightens, and keeps the whole Christian church on earth.

5 JESUS INSTITUTED HOLY BAPTISM AND THE LORD'S SUPPER (MATTHEW 3:13-17; 26:26-29).

The sacraments are called the *means of grace*. Along with our faith, the sacraments are effective and essential for our salvation (Mark 16:16). Through the sacraments and the spoken Word, we experience regeneration in the Holy Spirit (Titus 3:5-8).

6 THE CHURCH IS AN INCLUSIVE FELLOWSHIP (EPHESIANS 4:4-6).

The church gathers for worship, witness, and service (Romans 15:7). Through the proclamation of the Word and the administration of the sacraments, the church carries out the creative, redeeming, and sanctifying mission of God in the world (Matthew 28:16-20).

7 CHRIST WILL ONE DAY RETURN IN POWER TO JUDGE THE LIVING AND THE DEAD (MATTHEW 25:31FF).

It is the privilege of believers to be assured of their salvation and to live daily in the light of Christ's love (Romans 13:11-14).

BE AWARE

] These seven teachings do not constitute *everything* a Lutheran should be familiar with about the Bible, but they're a very good start.

TEN COMMON OCCUPATIONS IN BIBLE TIMES

1 SHEPHERD

Shepherds had a mixed reputation, as they worked far from home and were unable to keep many of the ritual laws. Israel's most famous king, David, was discovered while tending his father's sheep. Lamb was the most common entrée of the day.

2 SERVANT/SLAVE

Servants provided household duties and provided menial labor. Israel's release from slavery in Egypt is remembered as the saving event in Exodus. As a model for his followers, Jesus acted as a servant when washing the disciples' feet. At Jesus' time, roughly one-third of the region's population was enslaved.

Perhaps the most common occupation in the Bible is that of shepherd.

3 WATER GATHERER

Women typically gathered the household water each day, carrying jugs in the early morning and evening. Isaac's servant discovered Rebekah as she came with a jug of water, and Jesus revealed himself as Messiah to the Samaritan woman at the well.

4 FISHERMAN

Fish put food on the table and provided a source of income. Jesus called his first disciples, Peter, Andrew, James, and John, from their boats on the Sea of Galilee.

5 FARMER/VINTNER

Agriculture was the basis for the economy in the Bible. Crops included olives, wheat, barley, dates, grapes, and figs. Jesus used many farming and wine-based images in his teachings.

A third of the region's population was enslaved during Jesus' time, which is why it's such a common occupation in the Bible.

6 PRIEST

Priests served as mediators between God and the people in rituals of prayer and sacrifice. During the time of the temple, they ensured that the laws governing worship were carried out. Zechariah was keeping the oil lamps lit when, after scaring him, the angel announced the birth of his son, John the Baptist.

7 JUDGE

Judges were assembled once Israel was formed into tribes before the time of kings. They were like chieftains that resolved disputes and even fought battles. Famous judges include Deborah, Gideon, and Samson.

The climate in Bible lands is ideal for growing grapes, and wine was a safe, plentiful beverage. Consequently, vintner became a common occupation.

BIBLE STUFF

8 PROPHET

Prophets were designated by kings or called directly by the Lord. They were considered the conscience of the people who spoke God's word.

9 FOOD PREPARER

Women and servants spent much of the day in food-related tasks. Sarah prepared barley cakes for the three strangers visiting at Mamre. And Martha was working in the kitchen while Mary was learning from Jesus.

10 KING

Kings were responsible for Israel's well-being and faithfulness to God. Israel's first king was Saul, followed by David. David's son Solomon was the wealthiest of all the kings and built the first temple.

TOP 10 PRAYERS UTTERED IN THE BIBLE

OLD TESTAMENT

1 ABRAHAM'S PRAYER FOR SODOM (GENESIS 18:16-33)

Abraham's prayer on behalf of the people of Sodom focuses on the character of God rather than on the inhospitality and sin of the people of Sodom.

2 MOSES' PRAYER FOR ISRAEL IN THE WILDERNESS (EXODUS 32:9-14)

In this momentous prayer, Moses changed the mind of God from the destruction God had planned. Moses' prayer preserved the people of Israel.

3 SOLOMON'S PRAYER OF DEDICATION OF THE TEMPLE (2 CHRONICLES 6:1—7:4)

Solomon praised God for being present in the temple and on the earth among sinful people. This prayer of dedication and praise gives profound thanks to God.

4 DAVID'S PSALM OF SURRENDER (PSALM 139)

After coming face to face with God's intimate knowledge of him even in his mother's womb, David offers a prayer of surrender to God's searching, knowing, and refining ways.

5 DANIEL'S CONFESSION ON BEHALF OF HIS PEOPLE (DANIEL 9:1-19)

Daniel pleads with God to bring his people to their land even though they had rebelled. His hope was that God would be merciful and that the people would be deeply thankful.

In 67 B.C.E. the Romans conquered the Holy Land, but the Old Testament books had pretty much been completed by then anyway.

NEW TESTAMENT

6 THE LORD'S PRAYER (MATTHEW 6:5-15)

Jesus' teaching on prayer includes the Lord's Prayer as a pattern of being able to go to God with our needs, our struggles, and our praise.

7 JESUS' PRAYER FOR HIS DISCIPLES (JOHN 17:1-26)

Often called "The High Priestly Prayer," this wonderful prayer emphasizes that eternal life comes by knowing God through Jesus Christ. Jesus prays that his followers be one, just as he, the Father, and the Holy Spirit are One.

8 JESUS' PRAYER IN THE GARDEN OF GETHSEMANE (MATTHEW 26:36-45)

Jesus' agony in the garden helps us know that he experienced the depth of human suffering, but he was committed to leave his life in God's hands.

9 PAUL'S PRAYER FOR THE EPHESIANS (EPHESIANS 1:15-23; 3:14-21)

In this magnificent prayer Paul prays for the Ephesians to comprehend and embrace the heights and depths of God's amazing grace and love.

10 THE PRAYER OF THE GREAT MULTITUDE (REVELATION 19:1-10)

At the heart of worship is praise. This prayer, from the end of the Bible, is the triumphant roar of a great multitude in praise and worship.

BIBLE STUFF

A BRIEF HISTORY OF GOD'S COVENANT WITH THE PEOPLE

A covenant is a solemn exchange of promises between two parties. Five main biblical covenants reveal the history of God's relationship with the people, and these covenants often included signs. God always keeps promises, even though people rarely do.

1   COVENANT WITH NOAH

Because of human evil, God threatened to destroy human life with a great flood. But God repented of that intention and saved humanity and all his creation through Noah and his family. God then entered into a covenant with all living creatures and promised never again to destroy life on earth with a flood. As a sign of this promise, God put the rainbow in the sky.

2   COVENANT WITH ABRAHAM AND SARAH

God entered into a covenant with Abraham and Sarah so that their descendants would be "blessed to be a blessing." God promised that they would have many descendants and that the people would have a land to live in. As a sign of this promise, male Hebrew babies are circumcised.

3   COVENANT WITH MOSES AND ALL OF ISRAEL

After delivering the people from slavery in Egypt, God entered into a covenant with them. The Lord promised to be their God, and the people promised to be God's people. As part of the covenant, God gave the people the Ten Commandments and restored them to the land. As a sign of this covenant, God gave the Sabbath—one day off each week to rest from work and to spend time with God.

4 COVENANT WITH DAVID

David decided to build God a temple. God said, "No, I will build you a house," meaning a family tree. God promised King David that one of his descendants would forever rule over the people.

Interlude: The Promise of a New Covenant.
People are sinners. They did not keep the promises that they had made as part of their covenants with God. So through prophets such as Jeremiah and Ezekiel, God promised to make a new covenant.

5 THE NEW COVENANT

On the night in which he was betrayed, Jesus Christ made the new covenant. Through his death and resurrection, Jesus forgave all people for their sins and opened the way to eternal life for all. Through baptism, we become members of this covenant. Through Holy Communion, we are nourished in the covenant. The signs of the covenant are water, bread, and wine.

HOW TO READ KEY TYPES OF BIBLE LITERATURE

Like a newspaper, the Bible contains different types of writing gathered together in a single place. When reading a newspaper, readers make a mental adjustment based on the kind of material they're reading. You do not read the funnies the same way you read an advice column or a news story. The same thing goes for reading the Bible.

GENERAL GUIDELINES

] **Clarify the unclear bits first.**
One challenge of reading a Bible passage is to understand what it says on a basic level. Does the passage contain ancient terms or refer to ancient social practices that need clarification? Get the information clear before proceeding to higher meanings. Glossing over them will reduce the opportunity for God's word to reach you later on.

] **Ask of every passage you read, "What does this mean?"**
After clarifying exactly what a passage says, probe the meaning of the passage. Lutherans take their Bible reading cues from Martin Luther himself, a Bible scholar who demanded the highest standards of understanding for himself.

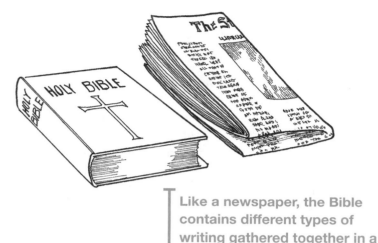

Like a newspaper, the Bible contains different types of writing gathered together in a single place.

A PSALM

] **Discern which type of psalm it is, then read it accordingly.**
A psalm is always a poem and is often a prayer. If the psalm is a prayer, read it as a prayer—words spoken to God. To the extent that the prayer fits your life, make it your own. For parts that do not fit your life, pray the prayer on behalf of other people.

] **Open yourself up to the psalm's teaching.**
The psalms are also poems of instruction; they teach us about God and ourselves. Explore the psalm as a poem, teasing out the meaning of its metaphors (such as God is a rock, or we are like trees) for your own life.

A PROPHETIC MESSAGE

The prophets were not predictors or prognosticators. They were messengers from God who brought God's word to specific times and places.

] **Learn the historical background.**
When reading a prophetic message, learn what you can about the time, place, and people to whom the message was sent (the notes in a good study Bible can help you do this). Learn what was going on that led God to send a message.

] **Apply the prophet's message to your own life.**
After understanding God's message as fully as possible, apply that message to yourself, your time, and your people.

A PARABLE

A parable is a short story designed to make a point. Jesus often used parables to teach and preach, often with a very specific message to a very specific audience.

] **Discern the original audience.**
When reading a parable, pay attention to whom Jesus addressed the parable. Was he telling the story to his disciples, or was he addressing his religious or political opponents? Keep this in mind when applying the story to yourself and your own time.

] **Balance Jesus' message from one parable with other lessons you learn.**
What you learn from a parable is just one of the many lessons available in the Bible. Be wary about drawing too big of a conclusion from just one parable.

A LETTER

] **Engage in active eavesdropping.**
When you read a letter (sometimes called an epistle), remember that you are reading someone else's mail. It is a little like listening in to one side of a phone conversation.

] **Avoid taking a portion out of context (known among Bible geeks as "proof-texting"). Use caution.**
In order to understand the part of the conversation you're reading, you have to work to place the little part of the conversation that you are overhearing within the larger conversation. Taking that smaller portion out of context can lead to all kinds of bad results.

A NARRATIVE ACCOUNT

] **Always take the big picture into account.**
When reading a portion of a narrative, try to place the part of the story that you are reading within the larger narrative. It is important to acknowledge that, as a reader, you know things about what is happening "behind the scenes" or about the ending of the story that the people in the story don't know yet.

] **Keep in mind who says what.**
If Jesus says something, you can bet it is true. But if the devil or a sinner says something, it may or may not be true.

A PROVERB

Proverbs are short, wise sayings meant to teach a practical lesson. There is a book of Proverbs in the Old Testament, but proverbs show up in other places too.

] **Take it for what it's worth.**
Proverbs often teach very practical things about daily life. They're not meant, however, to become slogans or personal mission statements that take over your life.

] **Consider memorizing proverbs you find meaningful for your life.**
Proverbs can add clarity in certain moments along the path. You may find the ones you memorize carry a theme that is particular to your situation or personality.

HOW TO INTERPRET "CONTROVERSIAL" BIBLE TEXTS AND REMAIN LUTHERAN

The Bible is filled with passages that are difficult to interpret or that people use in controversial ways. (The U.S. Supreme Court once used the Bible in a legal argument to defend and support slavery, for example.) Lutheran Christians inherit from our forebears some handy methods of figuring out how God is speaking to us through the Bible about tough contemporary issues, all while keeping our wits about us and the focus on Jesus Christ.

1 DISTINGUISH THE LAW FROM THE GOSPEL WITHIN THE PASSAGE.

One of the very first Lutheran documents says, "All Scripture should be divided into . . . the law and the promises."

- **The law:** The law is what God tells us to do for ourselves and for each other. Example: Love your neighbor.

- **The promise:** The promise, or gospel, is what God promises to do for us, because we cannot do it for ourselves. Example: Attain eternal life.

- **Which one?** We get into trouble when we confuse the two. When we expect God to do for us what God tells us to do (love your neighbor) or when we try to do for ourselves what only God can do for us (grant eternal life), we miss the mark.

2 ASK WHETHER THE PASSAGE IN QUESTION DELIVERS CHRIST.

Lutherans believe the Scriptures have authority because they "preach and inculcate [deliver] Christ. And this is the true test by which we judge all books, when we see whether they inculcate [deliver] Christ."

- **Delivering the true Christ:** Christ so loved the world that he laid down his life to save us. Is the passage being used by someone for some means other than preaching Christ as the savior of the world?

- **Let love be your guide:** Ask what a loving use of the Scripture passage would look like.

Some passages in the Bible can be controversial and difficult to comprehend in light of current events. Lutherans rely on their special method of carefully distinguishing the law from the gospel to make sense of things.

3 TEST THE PASSAGE TO SEE WHETHER IT IS ABOUT US, TODAY.

The Bible is filled with stories of God's people in different places and times. People sometimes pull a passage out of context and act as if God spoke the word through the radio today.

- For all times and places? Ask if the passage is a message for all times and places.

- **Sometimes "yes":** Sometimes passages do apply *directly* to us today. When Jesus says to love the Lord with all our hearts and love our neighbors as ourselves (Matthew 22:37-39), it is a good bet God means all of us all the time.

- **Sometimes "no":** Sometimes, passages apply *indirectly* to us today. Deuteronomy says, "When you build a new house, you shall make a parapet for your roof; otherwise you might bear bloodguilt on your house, if anyone should fall from it" (22:8), and it's a good bet that we need to apply this to our lives *indirectly.* But we do apply it to our lives.

4 ATTEMPT TO DISCERN THE ORIGINAL CONTEXT OF THE PASSAGE; AVOID COBBLING TOGETHER A FRACTURED MESSAGE FROM DISCRETE PARTS OF THE BIBLE.

Often, people connect the dots between very different passages and create a crazy line drawing.

- **Context, Part 1:** Figure out the context of the passage. Does reading the passage in its context help to clarify its meaning? If someone strings together more than one passage, are they using the different passages in a way that is faithful to original contexts?

- **Context, Part 2:** Figure out the context in which we are today. Are you using an ancient passage to support something in our culture that is contrary to God's will? Is there some sacred cow you are protecting by the use of this Scripture?

BE AWARE

] Lutherans believe strongly in a shared interpretation of the Bible. This means we tend to prefer figuring out what the Bible means for our time *together*, in conversation and honest debate, rather than simply allowing disagreements to resolve into conflict.

] Sometimes disagreements about the Bible can endure for long periods of time before events catch up.

THE EXODUS

God led the Israelites out of slavery in Egypt, through the wilderness, and to the promised land. Here is one possible route they took.

The promised land.

The exodus began here.

MEDITERRANEAN SEA

Lake Galilee

Jordan River

Mount Nebo

Jericho
Jerusalem ●
Gaza/ Hebron ●
Beersheba ●

NILE DELTA

ZIN DESERT

Zamorrah

DEAD SEA

Kadesh-Barnea

MOAB

Rameses

Succoth

SHUR DESERT

GOSHEN

Jothathah

Heliopolis ●   Pi-Hahiroth

SINAI PENNISULA

EDOM

● Memphis

PARAN DESERT

EGYPT

Marah

SIN DESERT

Ezion-Geber

Heracleopolis ●

Elim

Hazepoth

MIDIAN

NILE RIVER

Gulf of Suez

Gulf of Aqabah

● Akhetaton

Mount Sinai

RED SEA

Abydos ●

THE HOLY LAND—
OLD TESTAMENT TIMES

THE HOLY LAND—
NEW TESTAMENT TIMES

Sidon

PHOENICIA

LEBANON MTS.

ABILENE

Zarephath

Damascus

SYRIA

Mt. Hermon

Tyre

MEDITERRANEAN
SEA

Caesarea
Philippi

ITURAEA

GALILEE

Ptolemais

Caparnaum

BATANEA

LAKE
GALILEE

Mt. Carmel

Tiberias

AURANITIS

Nazareth

Dor

Mt. Tabor

SAMARIA

DECAPOLIS

Caesarea

Salim

Jordan River

Samaria

Mt. Ebai

Mt. Gerizim

Sychar

Gerasa

Joppa

Arimathea

Lydda

Ephraim

PEREA

Jabneel

Jericho

Philadelphia

Emmaus

Ashdad

Jerusalem

Bethany

Ascalon

Qumran

Bethlehem

Gaza

JUDEA

Hebron

DEAD
SEA

IDUMEA

Beersheba

NABATEA

JERUSALEM IN JESUS' TIME

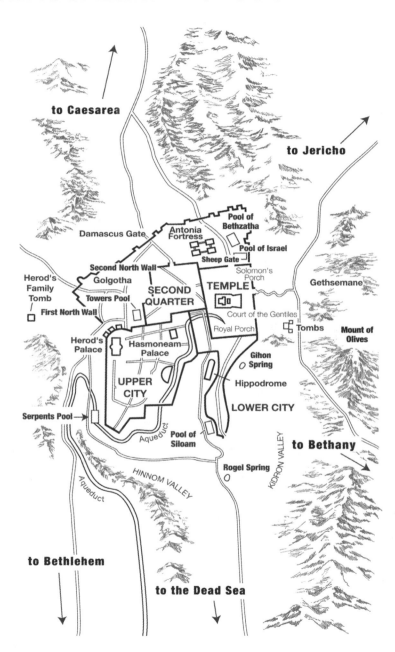

to Caesarea

to Jericho

Pool of Bethzatha

Damascus Gate

Antonia Fortress

Pool of Israel

Second North Wall

Sheep Gate

Solomon's Porch

Gethsemane

Herod's Family Tomb

Golgotha

Towers Pool

SECOND QUARTER

TEMPLE

First North Wall

Court of the Gentiles

Royal Porch

Tombs

Mount of Olives

Herod's Palace

Hasmoneam Palace

Gihon Spring

UPPER CITY

Hippodrome

LOWER CITY

Serpents Pool

Aqueduct

Pool of Siloam

to Bethany

HINNOM VALLEY

Rogel Spring

KIDRON VALLEY

Aqueduct

to Bethlehem

to the Dead Sea

NOAH'S ARK

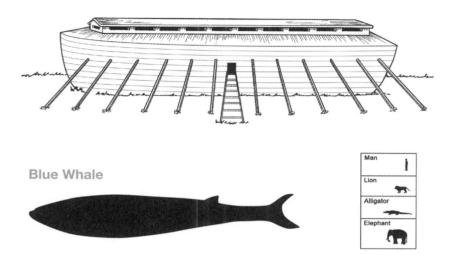

Blue Whale

Man	
Lion	
Alligator	
Elephant	

A cubit is equal to the length of a man's forearm from the elbow to the tip of the middle finger—approximately 18 inches or 45.7 centimeters. Noah's ark was 300 cubits long, 50 cubits wide, and 30 cubits tall (Genesis 6:15).

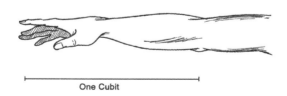

One Cubit

BIBLE STUFF

SOLOMON'S TEMPLE

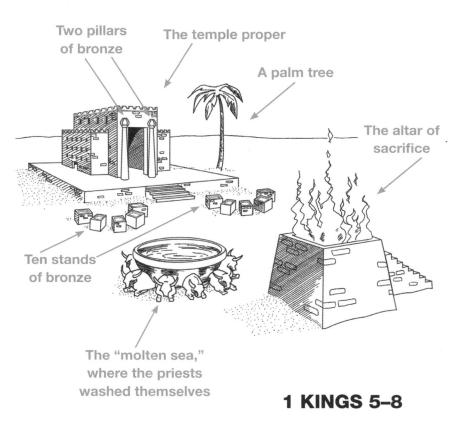

Two pillars of bronze

The temple proper

A palm tree

The altar of sacrifice

Ten stands of bronze

The "molten sea," where the priests washed themselves

1 KINGS 5–8

THE PASSION AND CRUCIFIXION

Judas betrayed Jesus with a kiss, saying, "the one I will kiss is the man; arrest him" (Matthew 26:48).

Unless you can read biblical Hebrew, Aramaic, and Greek, you might want to find yourself a good translation in a language you understand.

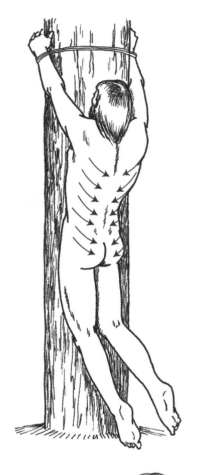

Jesus was flogged as part of his punishment. The pain would have been unbearable (Matthew 26:67).

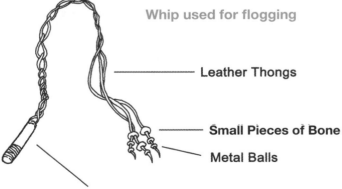

Whip used for flogging

Leather Thongs

Small Pieces of Bone

Metal Balls

Wooden Handle

After being flogged, carrying the patibulum was nearly impossible for Jesus.

Crucifixion was so common in Jesus' time that the Romans had special names for the parts of the cross.

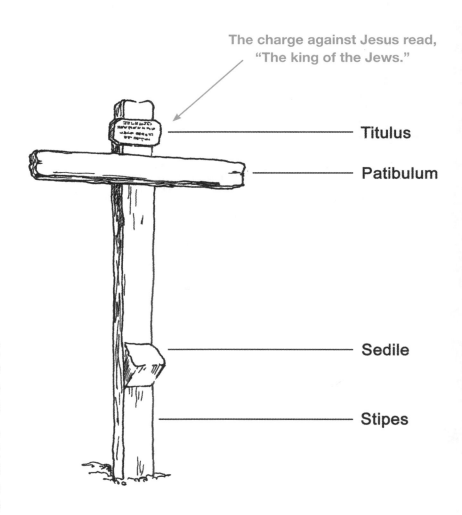

The charge against Jesus read, "The king of the Jews."

Titulus

Patibulum

Sedile

Stipes

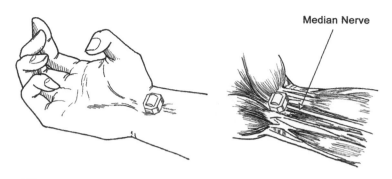

Median Nerve

Typical crucifixion involved being nailed to the cross through the wrists—an excruciatingly painful and humiliating punishment.

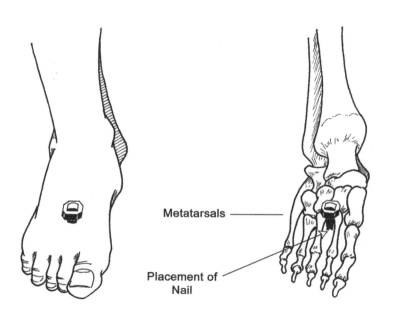

Metatarsals ————

Placement of
Nail

During a crucifixion, a single nail usually was used to pin both feet together to the cross.

Eventually, the victim would be unable to lift himself to take a breath, and he would suffocate.

While the Romans broke the legs of the men who were crucified next to Jesus, they found that Jesus had already died. To make sure, they pierced his side with a spear, probably to puncture his heart (John 19:34).

Joseph of Arimathea and several women took Jesus down and carried him to the tomb (Matthew 27:57–61).

The miracle of resurrection took place three days later, when Jesus rose from the dead.

CHURCH STUFF

Every well-prepared Lutheran should have a basic understanding of Lutheran teachings and where they came from.

Plus, since every church goes about worship in a slightly different way, it might take a little time to get the hang of things—especially if you're new to a congregation.

This section includes:

] Essential facts about the Lutheran faith. (If you know these things, you'll know more than most.)

] Practical advice for singing hymns, taking communion, and getting to know the people in your congregation.

] Hints for enjoying worship—even when you're having a bad day.

HOW TO RESPOND WHEN SOMEONE SITS IN YOUR PEW

We all carry a bubble of personal space. For some people, it's several feet. For others, it's about a millimeter. Wherever on the spectrum you happen to fall, there are certain situations in which we invite visitors into our little sphere of experience—like at church. Furthermore, human beings are territorial in nature and sometimes see strangers inside the bubble as an affront. These situations need not be cause for alarm.

1   **SMILE AND GREET THE "INTRUDERS."**
    Oftentimes they are visitors to your congregation—new blood. Avoid creating bad blood you might regret later on. Make solid eye contact so they know you mean it, shake hands with them, and leave no impression that they've done something wrong.

2   **VIEW THE "INTRUSION" AS AN OPPORTUNITY.**
    Remember, you don't own the pew; you just borrow it once a week. Take the opportunity to get out of your rut and sit someplace new. This will physically emphasize a change in your perspective and may yield new spiritual discoveries.

3   **IF YOU CAN TELL THAT YOUR NEW FRIENDS FEEL UNCOMFORTABLE AT HAVING DISPLACED YOU, DESPITE YOUR EFFORTS TO THE CONTRARY, MAKE AN EXTRA EFFORT TO WELCOME THEM.**
    Consider taking them to brunch after church to become acquainted. If there are too many for you to foot the bill, consider inviting them to accompany you on a "go Dutch" basis. This will eliminate any hierarchy and place you on equal footing.

HOW TO USE A WORSHIP BULLETIN

Many Lutheran congregations offer a printed resource called a bulletin to assist worshipers. The bulletin may contain the order of the service, liturgical information, music listings, the day's Bible readings, and important community announcements.

1 ARRIVE EARLY.
A few extra minutes before worship will allow you to scan the bulletin and prepare for the service.

2 RECEIVE THE BULLETIN FROM THE USHER.
Upon entering the worship space, an usher will give you a *bulletin*. Some congregations stack bulletins near the entrance for self-service.

3 REVIEW THE ORDER OF WORSHIP.
When seated, open the bulletin and find the order of the service, usually printed on the first or second page. Some churches print the entire service in the bulletin so worshipers don't have to switch back and forth between worship aids.

4 DETERMINE IF OTHER WORSHIP RESOURCES ARE REQUIRED.
The order of worship may specify additional hymnals, song sheets, candles, or other external supplies required during the service.

5 FILL OUT THE ATTENDANCE CARD.
A card may be located inside the bulletin or somewhere in your row. Fill it out completely. You may be asked to pass this card to an usher or to place it in the offering plate. Some congregations have visitors/communion attendance books for people to sign.

CHURCH STUFF

6 REFLECT ON BULLETIN ARTWORK.
Covers often feature a drawing or design that corresponds to the season of the church year or the day's Bible verses. Examine the artwork and make a note of its connection to the lessons or sermon.

7 TRACK YOUR WORSHIP PROGRESS.
The bulletin will guide you through the liturgy, hymns, and lessons as you worship and let you know where you are at all times.

8 WATCH FOR LITURGICAL DIALOGUES.
The bulletin may contain spoken parts of the liturgy not found in the hymnal. The worship leader's parts may be marked with a "P:" or "L:". The congregation's responses may be marked with a "C:" and are often printed in boldface type.

9 IDENTIFY THE WORSHIP LEADERS AND ASSISTANTS.
The names of ushers, musicians, greeters, readers, acolytes, and pastors usually can be found in the bulletin. Greet these people by name following the service. Make good eye contact.

10 REVIEW THE PRINTED ANNOUNCEMENTS.
Community activities, calendars, and updates are often listed in the back of the bulletin. Scan listings during the prelude music, the offering, or the spoken announcements.

11 MAKE GOOD USE OF THE BULLETIN AFTER THE SERVICE.
Some congregations re-use bulletins for later services. Return the bulletin if possible. Recycling bins may also be provided. If you wish, or unless otherwise instructed, you may take the bulletin home with you.

BE AWARE

] Bulletins often use letter or color codes to signify which hymnals should be used. Look for a key or legend that details this information.

] Many church secretaries and worship committees need help preparing the bulletin each week. You may want to volunteer to copy, fold, or assemble the bulletin for an upcoming service.

] Most congregations stand at certain times during worship, such as to honor Jesus' presence when the Gospel is read. Standing and sitting—even occasional kneeling—aren't for exercise. Rather, they're an important physical participation in worship that helps you focus on the meaning behind the action.

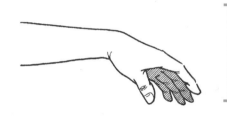

If you choose not to save your worship bulletin, be sure to recycle it whenever possible.

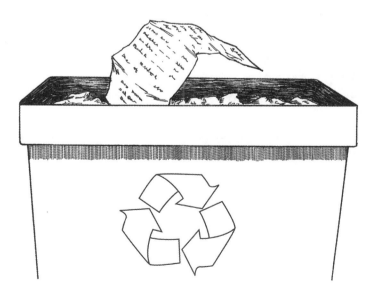

CHURCH STUFF

HOW TO SING A HYMN

Music is an important part of the Lutheran tradition and an enjoyable way to build community. Hymn singing can be done without demonstrable emotion, but many otherwise stoic Lutherans appropriately channel emotion into their hymn singing and are therefore loud.

1 LOCATE HYMNS IN ADVANCE.
As you prepare for worship, consult the worship bulletin or the hymn board to find numbers for the day's hymns. Bookmark these pages in the hymnal using an offering envelope or attendance card.

2 FAMILIARIZE YOURSELF WITH THE HYMNS.
Examine the composer credits, the years the composer(s) lived, and whether the tune has a different name than the hymn itself. Note how the hymn is categorized in the hymnal. Many hymnals group the songs into categories, such as "Society" and "Christmas."

3 ASSIST NEARBY VISITORS OR CHILDREN.
Using a hymnal can be confusing. If your neighbor seems disoriented, help them find the correct pages, or let them read from your book.

4 ADOPT A POSTURE FOR BEST VOCAL PERFORMANCE.
Hold the hymnal away from your body at chest level. Place one hand under the spine of the binding, leaving the other hand free to turn the pages. Keep your chin up so your voice projects outward.

5 BEGIN SINGING.

If the hymn is unfamiliar, sing the melody for the first verse. If you read music, explore the written harmony parts during the remaining verses. Loud-singing neighbors may or may not be in tune, so follow them with caution.

Support the hymnal's spine with one hand. Place the other on the open page.

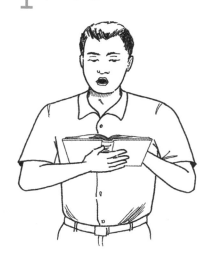

6 FOCUS ON THE HYMN'S CONTENT.

Some of the lyrics may connect with a scripture reading of the day. Certain ones may be especially inspiring.

7 AVOID DREARINESS.

Hymns are often sung in such a serious way that the congregation forgets to enjoy the music. Sing with energy and feeling.

BE AWARE

] Hymnals are not just for use at church. Consider keeping a personal copy of your congregation's hymnal at home for further reference and study. Hymnals also make excellent baptism or confirmation gifts.

] Some hymns use words and phrases that are difficult to understand (such as, "Here I raise my Ebenezer," from the hymn "Come, Thou Fount of Every Blessing"). Use a dictionary or a Bible with a concordance to clear up any uncertainty.

CHURCH STUFF

HOW TO SING A PRAISE SONG

Many Lutheran congregations use modern worship styles, often called Praise & Worship (P&W), featuring guitars and drums. In these settings the words are typically displayed on large, multi-media projection screens.

1 FOLLOW THE INSTRUCTIONS OF THE SONG LEADER.

Someone in the praise band will invite the congregation to stand up, sit down, repeat certain sections, or divide into men's and women's vocal parts. Pay attention to this person to avoid getting off track.

2 LEARN THE MELODY AND SONG STRUCTURE.

Pay special attention to the melody line sung by the band's lead vocalist. Praise & Worship songs can be tricky because they are rarely printed with notated sheet music and are sung differently from place to place.

3 SING ALONG WITH GUSTO.

Once the melody has been introduced, join in the singing. When you're comfortable with the song, experiment with harmony parts.

4 AVOID "ZONING OUT."

Singing lyrics that are projected on giant screens can result in a glazed-over facial expression. Avoid this by surveying the worship area, noticing paraments and liturgical symbols, and making eye contact with other people.

5 IDENTIFY LYRICAL THEMES.

Determine if the song is being used as a confession, a prayer, a hymn of praise, or serves another purpose.

6 WATCH OUT FOR RAISED HANDS.

Some Lutherans emote while singing contemporary Christian songs and may suddenly raise their hands in praise to God. Be sure to give these worshipers plenty of room to avoid losing your eyeglasses.

BE AWARE

] Lutheran worship is highly participatory. The praise band is there to help you and the congregation to sing and participate in worship, not to perform a concert.

] There are no strict prohibitions in the Lutheran tradition against physical expression during worship.

] In some congregations, praise gestures will draw amused stares.

Beware of especially passionate worshipers who might raise their hands too quickly.

CHURCH STUFF

THE ANATOMY OF A BAPTISM

Pastors preside at baptisms to ensure good order.

Pouring water on the baptized person, the pastor says, "I baptize you in the name of the Father, and of the Son, and of the Holy Spirit."

God is the true actor in baptism, bringing everyone involved to the font and inspiring trust and faith.

Sponsors (godparents) are on hand to support those being baptized and to make baptismal promises on behalf of children. The whole congregation joins in these promises and pledges their support also.

Typically a baptismal candle is lit and presented to show that the newly-baptized person has received the light of Christ. (Candle not shown.)

Note: Lutherans baptize people of all ages—not just infants.

After the baptism in water and God's word, the pastor traces the cross on the baptized person's forehead, often with anointing oil, and declares that he or she now belongs to Christ.

When children are baptized, their parents bring them to the font and make important promises to bring the child up in the Christian faith.

Baptism is received by a believing heart that trusts in God's word. In the case of infant baptism, the baptized person "borrows" one from his or her parents and sponsors.

Water is the earthly element in baptism. God uses it to wash away sin and to drown the "old Adam" or "old Eve" in the baptized person. Water in itself can't do it—baptism is water connected to the power of God's word, and it is received by God's gift of faith.

HOW TO LISTEN TO A SERMON

Lutherans believe God's Word comes to us through the sacraments and the preaching of Holy Scripture. Honoring God's Word, not to mention getting something out of church, includes diligent listening to the sermon and active mental participation.

1 REVIEW ACTIVE LISTENING SKILLS.
While the listener in this case doesn't get to speak, the sermon is still a conversation. Make mental notes as you listen. Take notice of where and why you react and which emotions you experience.

2 TAKE NOTES.
Note-taking promotes active listening and provides a good basis for later reflection. It also allows you to return to confusing or complicated parts at your own leisure. Some congregations provide space in the bulletin for notes, and many confirmation ministries provide structured worksheets.

Take notes to recall more information and get more out of the sermon.

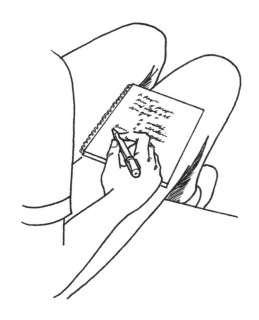

Try taking notes in an outline form so you can keep up without missing good information.

3   MAINTAIN GOOD POSTURE. AVOID SLOUCHING.
Sit upright with your feet planted firmly on the ground and your palms on your thighs. Beware of the impulse to slouch, cross your arms, or lean against your neighbor, as these can encourage drowsiness.

4   LISTEN FOR THE LAW.
You may feel an emotional pinch when the preacher names the sinner in you. Pay attention to your reaction, and try to focus on waiting for the gospel rather than becoming defensive. For more information, see "How to Tell the Difference Between the Law and the Gospel" on page 188.

5   LISTEN FOR THE GOSPEL.
This will come in the form of a sentence most likely starting with the name Jesus and ending with the words *for you*. Upon hearing the gospel, you may feel a physical lightness, as though you've set down a great burden. You may cry tears of joy. This is normal.

6 END BY SAYING, "AMEN."

Since preaching is mostly God's work, honor the Word by sealing the moment with this sacred word, which means, "It is most certainly true!"

7 REVIEW.

If you've taken written notes, read through them later that day or the next day and consider corresponding with the preacher if you have questions or need clarification. If you've taken mental notes, review them in a quiet moment. Consider sharing this review time with others in your congregation or household on a weekly basis.

HOW TO RECEIVE COMMUNION

The Sacrament of Holy Communion (sometimes called the Lord's Supper, the Eucharist, or simply the Meal) is a central event in Lutheran worship. All five senses are engaged in communion, and it is the most interactive part of the service. Local customs for receiving communion can be confusing or complex, so it's wise to pay attention and prepare.

1 **DETERMINE WHICH METHOD OF DISTRIBUTION IS USED.**
Verbal directions or printed instructions will likely be given prior to the distribution. The three most common methods for communion are *individual cups*, a *common cup*, or *intinction* (see pages 136–38).

Note: Some congregations commune at "tables" (gathered around the altar), and some practice "continuous communion" with bread and wine stations, and some do both.

2 **LOOK FOR GUIDANCE FROM THE USHER.**
The usher will direct the people in each row or pew to stand and get in line.

3 **PROCEED TO THE COMMUNION STATION.**
Best practice is often simply to follow the person in front of you and do what they do.

4 **KNEEL, IF APPROPRIATE.**
Congregations that commune at "tables" often do so by instructing communicants to kneel at an altar railing. When this happens, remember to stand slowly to avoid jostling your neighbor. Assist people who are elderly with altar rail navigation when they need help.

INDIVIDUAL CUPS

1 RECEIVE THE BREAD.
Extend your hands with palms facing up. After the server places the bread in your open hands, grasp the piece with the fingers of one hand. When the server says, "The body of Christ, given for you," eat the bread.

To receive the bread, make a "cross" or "cradle" with your hands, palms up.

Note: Bread is commonly distributed in both baked or "loaf" form and in wafer form. Either is acceptable.

2 RECEIVE THE WINE.
Take a filled cup from the tray. Some congregations provide a tray of empty cups as you come forward. If so, take one and hold it out to be filled by the server. When the server says, "The blood of Christ, shed for you," drink the wine.

3 RETURN THE EMPTY CUP.
A communion assistant may follow the servers with a tray for the used cups. Deposit your empty cup. It may be necessary for you to carry the empty cup over to a plate or basket located strategically on the way back to your seat.

COMMON CUP

1 RECEIVE THE BREAD.
See previous page.

2 RECEIVE THE WINE.
The wine will be served in a large cup or "chalice," as a sign of unity. Assist the server by placing one hand underneath the cup and the other hand on its side. Help the server guide the cup to your lips.

3 AVOID LEAVING BACKWASH.
Drink only one sip from the common cup. Remove your lips from the cup immediately after receiving the wine.

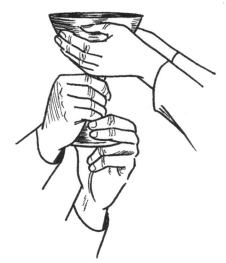

Use teamwork to receive the wine by common cup.

INTINCTION

Note: The word *intinction* is from the Latin word *intingere*, which means "to dip."

1 RECEIVE THE BREAD.
Follow the same procedure as with individual cups and common cup, but DO NOT EAT THE BREAD YET. If you accidentally eat the bread prematurely, REMAIN CALM. Simply ask for another piece.

CHURCH STUFF

2 RECEIVE THE WINE.

Position the bread you are holding over the cup. Grasp the bread tightly and dip just the edge of it into the wine. When the server says, "The blood of Christ shed for you," eat the wine-soaked bread.

3 DO NOT PANIC IF YOU ACCIDENTALLY DROP YOUR BREAD INTO THE CUP.

Again, the server can provide you with more bread. If the person distributing bread is too far away, the wine server may allow you to drink directly from the cup. Receiving only one element (bread *or* wine) counts as full participation in communion.

Gently dip the bread in the wine for communion by intinction.

ONCE YOU HAVE COMMUNED

] *Return to your seat.* If communion is distributed in one continuous line, you may immediately return to your pew.

OR

] *Wait for the completion of the distribution.* If you're being served as a group at the altar rail, you may need to wait until all other worshipers are served before returning to your seat. This is an appropriate time to close your eyes, pray, or listen to the communion music.

] *Receive the post-communion blessing.* When everyone has been served, the presiding minister may bless the group. You may make the sign of the cross during this blessing. (See illustration on page 206.)

] *Continue to participate when seated.* After returning to your place, you may join the congregation in singing the remaining communion hymns, or pray in silence.

CHURCH STUFF

BE AWARE

] When receiving the bread, place one upward palm on top of the other symbolically to make a "cross" or "cradle" with your hands.

] Many congregations offer the option of grape juice in addition to wine during communion. Verbal or written instructions will be given prior to distribution so you will be able to identify which chalice or cup contains grape juice.

] After receiving the bread and wine, avoid saying, "Thank you" to the server. The body and blood are gifts from God. If you wish, a gentle "Amen" is appropriate.

] Pastoral blessings are often available for children or adults who are not communing.

HOW TO PASS THE PLATE

Passing the offering plate requires physical flexibility and an ability to adapt to differing practices. The offering is a practice that dates back to Old Testament times, linking money and personal finance directly to one's identity as a child of God. Giving of one's financial resources is an integral part of a healthy faith life.

1 **PAY CLOSE ATTENTION TO INSTRUCTIONS, IF ANY.**
   The presiding minister may announce the method of offering, or instructions may be printed in the worship bulletin or projected on an overhead screen.

2 **BE ALERT FOR THE PLATE'S ARRIVAL AT YOUR ROW OR PEW.**
   Keep an eye on the ushers, if there are any. In most congregations, guiding and safeguarding the offering plate is their job, so wherever they are, so is the plate. As the plate approaches you, set aside other activity and prepare for passing.

3 **AVOID WATCHING YOUR NEIGHBOR OR MAKING JUDGMENTS ABOUT THEIR OFFERING.**
   Many people contribute once a month by mail and some by automatic withdrawal from a bank account. If your neighbor passes the plate to you without placing an envelope, check, or cash in it, do not assume they didn't contribute.

4 **PLACE YOUR OFFERING IN THE PLATE AS YOU PASS IT POLITELY TO THE NEXT PERSON.**
   Do not attempt to make change from the plate if your offering is in cash. Avoid letting the plate rest in your lap as you finish writing a check. Simply pass it on and hand your check to an usher as you leave at the end of worship.

5 BE SENSITIVE TO IDIOSYNCRASIES IN PLATE TYPES.

Some congregations use traditional, wide-rimmed, felt-lined, brass-plated offering plates. Some use baskets of varying types. Some use cloth bags hung at the ends of long wooden poles that the ushers extend inward from the ends of the pews.

THREE TYPICAL STYLES OF OFFERING PLATES

Brass offering plate

Plain offering basket

Offering basket on long pole

BE AWARE

] Some congregations place the offering plate or basket at the rear of the worship space.

] Your church offering may be tax deductible, as provided by law. Consider making your offering by check or automatic withdrawal; you will receive a statement from your church in the first quarter of the next year.

] Churches often depend entirely upon the money that comes in through congregational offerings. If you are a member, resolve to work yourself toward tithing as a putting-your-money-where-your-mouth-is expression of faith. (The term *tithing* means "one-tenth" and refers to the practice of giving 10 percent of one's gross income to support the church's work.)

] Everyone, regardless of their age, has something to offer.

] Offerings are not fees or dues given out of obligation. They are gifts of thanksgiving returned to God from the heart.

HOW TO SHARE THE PEACE IN CHURCH

In Romans 16:16, Paul tells members of the congregation to "greet one another with a holy kiss." The First Letter of Peter ends, "Greet one another with a kiss of love. Peace to all of you who are in Christ" (1 Peter 5:14).

Some Lutherans worry about this part of the worship service due to its free-for-all nature. Some also feel uncomfortable because of their fear of being hugged. You can survive the peace, however, with these steps.

1 **ADOPT A PEACEFUL FRAME OF MIND.**
Clear your mind of distracting and disrupting thoughts so you can participate joyfully and reverently.

2 **DETERMINE THE APPROPRIATE FORM OF SAFE TOUCH.**
Handshaking is most common. Be prepared, however, for hugs, half-hugs, one-armed hugs, pats, and other forms of physical contact. Nods are appropriate for distances greater than two pews or rows.

3 **REFRAIN FROM EXTRANEOUS CHITCHAT.**
The sharing of the peace is not the time for lengthy introductions to new people, comments about the weather, or observations about yesterday's game. A brief encounter is appropriate, but save conversations for the coffee hour.

4 **MAKE APPROPRIATE EYE CONTACT.**
Look the other person in the eye but do not stare. The action of looking the person in the eye highlights the relationship brothers and sisters in Christ have with one another.

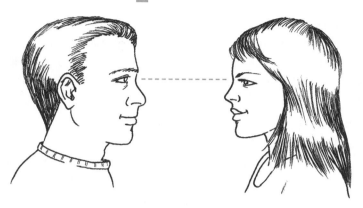

5 DECLARE THE PEACE OF GOD.
"The peace of the Lord be with you," "Peace be with you,"
"The peace of God," "God's peace," and "The peace of
Christ," are ways of speaking the peace. Once spoken, the
peace is there. Move on to the next person.

BE AWARE

] Safe touch involves contact that occurs within your personal
space but does not cause discomfort or unease.

CHURCH STUFF

HOW TO STAY ALERT IN CHURCH

1 **GET ADEQUATE SLEEP.**
Late Saturday nights are Sunday morning's worst enemy.
Resolve to turn in earlier. A good night's sleep on Friday night
is equally important to waking rested on Sunday, as sleep
debt builds up over time.

2 **DRINK PLENTY OF WATER, THOUGH NOT TOO MUCH.**
It is easier to remain alert when you are well hydrated. Consider keeping a small bottle of water with you during worship.
One quick bathroom break is considered permissible. Two or
more are bad form.

3 **EAT A HIGH-PROTEIN BREAKFAST.**
Foods high in carbohydrates force your body to metabolize
them into sugars, which can make you drowsy. If your diet
allows, eat foods high in protein instead, such as scrambled
eggs with bacon.

4 **ARRIVE EARLY AND FIND THE COFFEE POT.**
If you don't drink coffee, consider a caffeinated soda.

5 **FOCUS ON YOUR POSTURE.**
Sit up straight with your feet planted firmly on the floor. Avoid
slouching, as this encourages sleepiness. Good posture will
promote an alert bearing and assist in paying attention, so
you'll get more out of worship.

6 **IF YOU HAVE DIFFICULTY FOCUSING ON THE SERVICE, DIVERT YOUR ATTENTION. OCCUPY YOUR MIND, NOT YOUR HANDS.**
Look around the worship space for visual stimuli. Keep your
mind active in this way while continuing to listen.

7 STAY ALERT BY FLEXING MUSCLE GROUPS IN A PATTERN.

Clench toes and feet; flex calf muscles, thighs, glutei, abdomen, hands, arms, chest, and shoulders. Repeat. Avoid shaking, rocking, or other movements that attract undue attention.

8 IF ALL ELSE FAILS, CONSIDER PINCHING YOURSELF.

Dig your nails into the fleshy part of your arm or leg, pinch yourself, bite down on your tongue with moderate pressure. Try not to cry out.

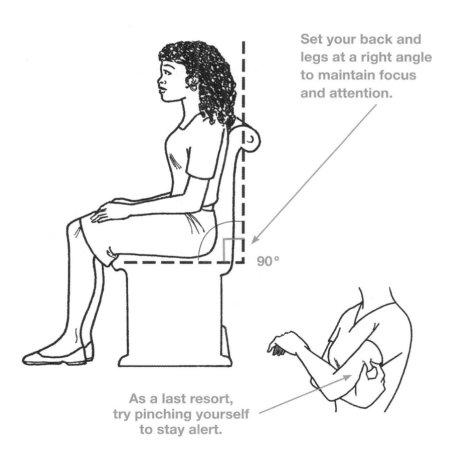

Set your back and legs at a right angle to maintain focus and attention.

90°

As a last resort, try pinching yourself to stay alert.

WHAT TO BRING TO A CHURCH POTLUCK (BY REGION)

It is a generally followed practice in North American churches to enjoy three courses at potlucks (commonly referred to as "dishes"). Many of these dishes take on the flavor of the regions or cultures they represent. For best results, the preparer should understand the context in which the "dish" is presented.

THE SALAD

Potluck salads are quite different from actual salads. In preparation for making a potluck salad, ask yourself three questions:

] Is this dish mostly meat-free?

] Can this dish be served with a spoon or salad tongs?

] Can it be served chilled?

If the answer is "yes" to any of these questions, consider the dish a potluck-eligible salad.

THE MIXTURE

This is the foundation of any potluck salad. It gives the salad a sense of direction. If at all possible, use ingredients that are indigenous to your area. For example, broccoli, lettuce, apples, macaroni, and candy bars are common in more temperate climates.

THE CRUNCHY STUFF

This component gives life and pizzazz to an otherwise bland salad. Examples: tortilla chips, shoestring potato crisps, onion crisps, and fried pigskins.

THE GLUE

The glue holds the salad together. The variety of available types is stunning, ranging from a traditional oil-based salad dressing to mayonnaise and non-dairy whipped topping. Use your imagination. Consult regional recipes for exact ingredients.

Note: Some salads are best when made well in advance and allowed to sit overnight. This is called *marinating*, or "controlled decomposition." Do not use actual glue adhesive. Other salads are best prepared immediately before serving.

THE CASSEROLE

A three-layered dish, typically. In order to make each casserole as culturally relevant as possible, use the following guidelines. Consult local restaurants for ideas, when in doubt.

STARCH

East Coast: pasta or rice pilaf

Midwest: rice, potatoes, noodles, or more rice

South: grits

Southwest: black, red, or pinto beans

West Coast: tofu

MEAT

East Coast: sausage or pheasant

Midwest: ground beef—in a pinch, SPAM® luncheon meat

South: crawdad or marlin

Southwest: pulled pork

West Coast: tofu

CEREAL

East Coast: corn flakes

Midwest: corn flakes

South: corn flakes

Southwest: corn flakes

West Coast: tofu flakes

Note: The starch and meat may be mixed with a cream-based soup. The cereal must always be placed on the top of the casserole.

Salad

Casserole

Dessert

STUDENT BOOK

THE DESSERT

The most highly valued dish at a potluck, this can be the simplest and most fun to make. There are two key ingredients:

1. flour

2. fudge

Regional influences can be quite profound. The following are examples of typical desserts around the country. Consult your church's seniors for the nuances of your region.

Cleveland: fudge brownies with fudge frosting

Kansas City: triple-fudge fudge with fudge sauce and a side of fudge

Los Angeles: tofu fudge

Miami: fudge

New York City: cheesecake with fudge drizzle

BE AWARE

] Use caution when preparing a dish. Adding local ingredients to any meat, salad, or dessert can increase the fellowship factor of your potluck exponentially. It also raises the risk of a "flop."

] Always follow safe food-handling guidelines.

] Any combination of flavored gelatin, shredded carrots, mini-marshmallows, and canned pears is an acceptable "utility" dish, should you be unable to prepare one from the above categories.

LUTHER'S GERMANY

1483   Martin Luther is born on November 10 in Eisleben,
            Germany. He is the son of Hans and Margarethe Luther.

1488–1497   Young Martin attends school in Mansfeld.

1497–1498   He attends school in Magdeburg.

1498–1501   He attends school in Eisenach.

1501–1505   Martin Luther studies at Erfurt University and gradu-
            ates with an M.A. degree (master of the seven
            liberal arts). At his father's request, he switches to
            jurisprudence.

1505   On July 2, Luther is overtaken by a thunderstorm
            near Stotternheim. When lightning strikes nearby, he
            vows to become a monk. On July 17, he enters the
            Monastery of the Augustinian Mendicant Friars in
            Erfurt.

1507   Luther is ordained as a priest.

1508–1510   He lectures on philosophy and theology in Witten-
            berg and Erfurt.

1510/1511   He travels to Rome on matters concerning the
            Augustinian Order.

1512   Luther becomes professor of theology and lecturer in
            interpretation of the Scriptures at Wittenberg Univer-
            sity. From 1513–1518, he gives important lectures
            on the book of Psalms and the letters to Romans,
            Galatians, and Hebrews.

1517   On October 31, Luther nails his Ninety-five Theses
            denouncing the dispensation of indulgences to the
            door of the palace church in Wittenberg.

1518   On October 12-14, he is interrogated by Cardinal
            Cajetan in Augsburg.

1519 In June and July, the disputation with Eck in Leipzig, during which time Luther challenges the pope's infallibility.

1520/1521 Three of Luther's major works on the Reformation are published: "To the Christian Nobility of the German Nation," "On the Freedom of a Christian Person," and "On the Babylonian Captivity of the Church."

1520 Luther burns the Canon Law and the Papal bull of condemnation in front of the Elster Gate in Wittenberg.

1521 On January 3, Luther is excommunicated by the pope. On April 17-18, Luther defends himself before the Imperial Diet in Worms. He refuses to recant, as demanded by the Emperor Karl V, and is banned by him.

1521–1522	Luther is rescued by the Elector Frederick the Wise and taken to the Wartburg where, disguised as Junker Jörg, he translates the New Testament.
1522	Luther returns to Wittenberg.
1525	Nürnberg becomes the first imperial town to adopt the Reformation. That year, Martin Luther marries a former nun, Katharina von Bora. They have three sons and three daughters in the years that follow.
1529	By this time, Luther finishes compiling the Large and Small Catechisms.
1530	Martin Luther, Philip Melanchthon, Justus Jonas, and Johannes Bugenhagen compile the Torgau Articles, which form the basis of the Augsburg Confession. Luther stays in Coburg Fortress during the Imperial Diet in Augsburg.
1534	Luther's translation of the entire Old and New Testaments appears in print.
1537	In Schmalkalden, at the instigation of the Elector Frederick the Magnanimous, Luther compiles the "Schmalkalden Articles" (the main elements of the advice proffered to the league of Protestant towns and princes).
1544	The consecration by Luther of the palace church in Torgau, the first Protestant ecclesiatical building.
1545/1546	Luther pays three visits to his original home in order to settle legal disputes between the counts of Mansfeld.
1546	Martin Luther dies in Eisleben on February 18. He is buried in the palace church in Wittenberg on February 22.

SEVEN IMPORTANT THINGS LUTHER SAID (AND ONE FUNNY ONE) AND WHAT THEY MEANT

1 "WHEN OUR LORD AND MASTER, JESUS CHRIST, SAID, 'REPENT,' [MATTHEW 4:17] HE CALLED FOR THE ENTIRE LIFE OF BELIEVERS TO BE ONE OF REPENTANCE."

—Ninety-five Theses (1517)

Luther meant that faith and its Christly acts of love and service are never to be separated from real life. Faith isn't just a hobby, it's an entire way of life!

2 "THE LAW SAYS, 'DO THIS,' AND IT'S NEVER DONE. GRACE SAYS, 'BELIEVE IN THIS,' AND EVERYTHING IS ALREADY DONE."

—Heidelberg Disputation (1518)

This statement highlights how important Martin Luther believed it to be that Christians understand the difference between God's law and the gospel. A life free to serve others begins with this. No matter how well you keep the law, only the free gift of the gospel can save you.

3 "A CHRISTIAN IS A PERFECTLY FREE LORD OF ALL, SUBJECT TO NONE. A CHRISTIAN IS A PERFECTLY DUTIFUL SERVANT OF ALL, SUBJECT TO ALL."

—The Freedom of a Christian (1520)

By this, Luther meant that Jesus Christ is a Christian's only Lord—a Lord who commands us to love our neighbor as we love ourselves.

4 **"UNLESS I AM CONVINCED BY THE TESTIMONY OF THE SCRIPTURES OR BY CLEAR REASON . . . I AM BOUND BY THE SCRIPTURES I HAVE QUOTED AND MY CONSCIENCE IS CAPTIVE TO THE WORD OF GOD. I CANNOT AND I WILL NOT RETRACT ANYTHING, SINCE IT IS NEITHER SAFE NOR RIGHT TO GO AGAINST CONSCIENCE. I CANNOT DO OTHERWISE, HERE I STAND, MAY GOD HELP ME, AMEN."**

—*Speech at the Diet of Worms* (April 15, 1521)

With this bold and defiant statement, Martin Luther drew a line in the sand and started an age of reformation for the Christian church.

5 **"BE A SINNER AND SIN BOLDLY, BUT BELIEVE AND REJOICE IN CHRIST EVEN MORE BOLDLY, FOR HE IS VICTORIOUS OVER SIN, DEATH, AND THE WORLD."**

—*Letter to Philip Melanchthon* (August 1, 1521)

Jesus came to save sinners. There's no point in denying you're a sinner. But more importantly, knowing you're a sinner will bring you closer to Jesus Christ, the one person who can save you from sin and death.

6 **"THIS IS MOST CERTAINLY TRUE."**

—*Small Catechism* (1529)

The freedom God declares through Jesus Christ can be fully believed and should not be doubted. Luther wanted the word *Amen* to be spoken with complete confidence.

It's true. We're beggars

I Martin Luther's last
written words.

7 **"IT'S TRUE. WE'RE BEGGARS."**
—*Luther's last written words* (February 16, 1546)

This is Luther's final testimony to humankind's total dependence on the grace and mercy of God and to life's character as an absolute gift.

8 **"YOUR MANURE CURE DIDN'T HELP ME EITHER."**
—*Letter to Katie Luther* (1537)

Medieval home remedies for skin rashes weren't always what they were cracked up to be. Luther tried one of his wife's, and apparently it didn't work.

CHURCH STUFF

THE MOST OUTRAGEOUS LUTHER QUOTES AND WHAT THEY MEAN

1 **"A 'GOD' IS THE THING WE LOOK TO FOR ALL GOOD AND WHERE WE TRY TO FIND REFUGE WHEN WE'RE IN NEED."** *(THE LARGE CATECHISM)*
   The thing in your life you most trust or fear losing is your god. It can be your health, status, control, or continuing existence, among other things. All statements about sin revolve around whom you ultimately trust. God wants to be that one.

2 **"SIN BOLDLY."** *(LETTER TO PHILIP MELANCHTHON)*
   Christianity isn't for good people. It's for sinners. So Luther encouraged people to fess up to their sinfulness and then trust even more in Christ's mercy. (See page 156 for a complete quote.)

3 **"THE JEWS ARE ACTUALLY CLOSER TO CHRIST THAN WE ARE."** *(THAT JESUS CHRIST WAS BORN A JEW)*
   In contrast to his often quoted words against the Jews, Luther argued here that we ought to respect Jewish people as chosen by God and regard ourselves as adopted into the family through Christ's death and resurrection.

4 **"THE HUMAN WILL IS PLACED BETWEEN GOD AND THE DEVIL LIKE A BEAST OF BURDEN."** *(BONDAGE OF THE WILL)*
   Free will is an illusion. Our will is controlled either by God or the devil. God takes the reins whenever the Word brings faith.

5 **"A THEOLOGIAN OF THE CROSS TEACHES THAT PUNISHMENTS, CROSSES, AND DEATH ARE THE MOST PRECIOUS SAVINGS ACCOUNT OF ALL."** *(EXPLANATIONS OF THE NINETY-FIVE THESES)*
Salvation is best encountered in places where God first seems absent, rather than in power, success, and glory. That's where our cross is joined to Christ's.

6 **"WHEN YOU HAVE FAITH YOU HAVE TO STICK WITH CHRIST INCARNATE IN THE MANGER. IF YOU WANT TO CLIMB HIGHER AND TAKE A LOOK AT OUR LORD GOD'S WORK, YOU'LL FALL."** *(COMMENTARY ON ISAIAH 66:1)*
God reveals God's self in Christ Jesus, and that's where we ought to look. Without him, you'll never find anything but terror or a mirror image of yourself.

7 **"I STOMP ALL OVER REASON AND ITS WISDOM AND SAY, 'SHUT UP, YOU CURSED WHORE! ARE YOU TRYING TO SEDUCE ME INTO COMMITTING FORNICATION WITH THE DEVIL?'"** *(THE LAST SERMON IN WITTENBERG)*
Theology that serves as its own end does no one any good and ought to be condemned. But theology that serves to preach the gospel in its truth and purity is theology properly done.

8 **"GOOD, MODEST CHURCHES WITH LOW ARCHES ARE THE BEST FOR PREACHERS AND FOR LISTENERS, FOR THE ULTIMATE REASON FOR THESE BUILDINGS ISN'T THE BELLOWING AND BAWLING OF CHOIR MEMBERS BUT THE WORD OF GOD AND ITS PROCLAMATION."** *(TABLE TALK, 3781)*
A sanctuary right out of *Better Divine Homes and Churches* may be nice to look at, but if the law and gospel aren't heard there it's missing the point. A good sound system beats beautiful architecture hands down.

9 "WOMEN AND MAIDENS HAVE STARTED BARING THEMSELVES IN FRONT AND BACK, AND THERE ISN'T ANYONE WHO PUNISHES OR OBJECTS." *(LETTER TO KATIE LUTHER, 1545)*

Things were never this bad in my day. What is this generation coming to?

10 "I DON'T KNOW ANY OTHER COMFORT, HELP, OR COUNSEL FOR MY SALVATION EXCEPT THAT CHRIST IS MY MERCY SEAT." *(SERMON ON THE SUM OF THE CHRISTIAN LIFE)*

Sinners always want to look for something other than Christ to bring them salvation. But Luther proclaims that Christ's mercy is more than enough—it's everything.

Luther asserted that churches with low arches are best because they facilitate the preaching and hearing of God's word.

A BRIEF HISTORY
OF THE LUTHERAN MOVEMENT

Martin Luther didn't like the fact that his "followers" were being called Lutherans: "How is it that I—poor, stinking bag of maggots that I am—should have people call the children of Christ by my wretched name?" For better or worse, the "Lutheran" moniker stuck. Here's a brief history of the Lutheran movement and its continuing spread.

1483   Martin Luther born in Eisleben, Germany.

1505   Luther quits law school and enters the monastery.

1512   Luther begins teaching at Wittenberg University, lecturing on the Bible.

1517   Luther posts the *Ninety-five Theses on the Power and Efficacy of Indulgences.*

1518   Philipp Melanchthon joins the Wittenberg faculty.

1521   Luther's famous stand at the Diet of Worms.

1523   The first Lutheran martyrs: Two Lutheran monks burned at the stake in Brussels.

        King Gustavus Vasa begins spread of Lutheran movement to Sweden and Finland.

1529   Small and Large Catechisms published.

        Lutherans debate Zwinglians at Marburg; subject: Where's Jesus in the Lord's Supper?

        Lutherans and other reformers labeled "Protestants" as Diet of Speier.

1530	Melanchthon drafts the Augsburg Confession (presented at the Diet of Augsburg).

Later, Melanchthon publishes a defense (*Apologia*) of the articles of the Augsburg Confession. |
| 1537 | Two more Confessional Documents, *The Smalcald Articles* (by Luther) and *On the Power and Primacy of the Pope* (by Melanchthon) are published.

Denmark becomes officially Lutheran (and with it, eventually, Norway). |
1546	Luther dies in Eisleben.
1548	The controversial "Leipzig Interim" attempts a compromise with Rome in the face of the Smalcald War begun earlier that year.
1555	"The Peace of Augsburg" allows territorial rulers to establish either the Lutheran or Roman Catholic confession in their lands (this according to the principle of *cuius regio eius religio* = "whose territory, his religion").
1560	Melanchthon dies in Wittenberg.
1580	"The Formula of Concord" is published in attempt to settle inter-Lutheran disputes once and for all. Nice try. The "Formula" is included in *The Book of Concord,* which includes the Augsburg Confession and other key Lutheran documents. *The Book of Concord* helps usher in a period of "Lutheran Orthodoxy" in Germany.
1620	Rasmus Jensen, the first Lutheran pastor sent to the "New World" (from Denmark) dies near what is now Churchill, Manitoba.

1648   "The Peace of Westphalia" ends the brutal Thirty Years War between various Protestant and Roman Catholic forces.

1649   First Lutheran Church, Albany, New York, founded by Dutch settlers; it is the first officially organized Lutheran church in what would become the United States.

1675   Philip Jacob Spener's little book *Pia Desideria* ("Pious Desires") launches the Pietist movement. The subtitle of his book describes this movement well: "Heartfelt Yearnings for the God-pleasing Improvement of the True Evangelical Church."

1723   Johann Sebastian Bach becomes Director of Music in Leipzig; for Lutherans, Bach represents the epitome of combining sound biblical theology with the church's worship and choral music (see Bach's *St. Matthew's Passion*).

1817   In an early attempt at enforced ecumenism, King Frederick William III organizes Lutheran and Reformed Christians into the "Prussian Union."

1847   German immigrant and pastor C. F. W. Walther named first president of the newly formed Lutheran Church–Missouri Synod.

1933   In response to the formation of Hitler's Reich Church, pastors like Dietrich Bonhoeffer and Martin Niemöller form the underground "Confessing Church."

1947   The Lutheran World Federation (LWF) is organized in the aftermath of World War II. In 2006, the LWF membership included 140 different Lutheran church bodies, in 78 different countries, representing about 66 million Lutheran Christians.

1987   The Evangelical Lutheran Church in America is formed; the ELCA represents a merger of predecessor Lutheran churches of primarily Swedish, Norwegian, and German heritage.

The history of the Lutheran movement is rich with colorful characters and inspiring stories. C. F. W. Walther was the first president of the Missouri Synod and wore bushy sideburns and a neck beard, which were fashionable in 1847.

FIVE THINGS YOU SHOULD KNOW ABOUT THE LUTHERAN REFORMATION

1 **MOST PEOPLE IN MEDIEVAL TIMES HAD LOW EXPECTATIONS.**
They didn't know anything about advanced medicine, modern psychology, or what it was like to live in a democracy. They didn't expect to live very long. They didn't think they had much power over their lives. And they didn't think being an "individual" was very important.

2 **THE "LUTHERAN" REFORMERS WERE CATHOLIC.**
The reformers wanted to make changes within the one Christian church in Europe, but they wanted to stay Catholic. None of them ever expected that their actions would lead to the dozens of Christian denominations around today.

3 **PEOPLE IN MEDIEVAL TIMES WEREN'T ALLOWED TO CHOOSE THEIR OWN RELIGION.**
You could believe whatever you wanted, but you could only practice the faith your prince or king chose. After the Reformation, only the regions whose princes had signed the Augsburg Confession could practice any faith other than Catholicism.

4 **MARTIN LUTHER WASN'T THE ONLY REFORMER.**
Luther wanted the church to rediscover the good news of Jesus that creates and restores faith. Other reformers fought for these changes: separation of church and state, a mystical relationship with God, better-educated priests, and more moral leaders in the church.

5 **LUTHER AND HIS COLLEAGUES CARED ABOUT WHAT YOU HEAR IN CHURCH TODAY.**
They taught pastors how to tell the difference between law and gospel so the Word of God would hit home and create faith. This skill has been taught to Lutheran pastors ever since.

FIVE IMPORTANT THINGS THE LUTHERAN REFORMERS WROTE (OR TRANSLATED) AND WHY THEY'RE STILL IMPORTANT TODAY

1 THE AUGSBURG CONFESSION

In 1530, the Holy Roman Emperor called the Lutheran reformers to the city of Augsburg, Germany, to defend their teachings. The document they presented became known as the Augsburg Confession. It is mentioned in every Lutheran congregation's constitution to this day. The Augsburg Confession shows how the reformers talked about God's love for sinners. It also depicts how Lutherans organized themselves to make sure God's promises can be proclaimed.

2 THE SMALL AND LARGE CATECHISMS

Martin Luther led a team of people to see how well congregations were doing making sure people got the good news of Jesus. They found that many Christians in their territories didn't know the most basic parts of the faith. Luther wrote the Small Catechism so families would have a handy summary of the Christian faith. He wrote the Large Catechism so pastors could learn to preach so that people would have faith.

CHURCH STUFF

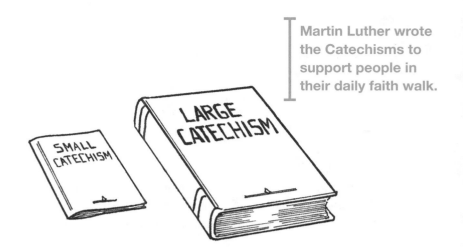

Martin Luther wrote the Catechisms to support people in their daily faith walk.

3   LUTHER'S "SEPTEMBER TESTAMENT"

In Luther's time, most people never read the Bible because most copies were written in Latin, a language that no one spoke and few Germans could even read. Luther changed this by translating the New Testament into German. The first edition became known as the "September Testament" because it was printed in September 1522. By translating Scripture into German, Luther returned the New Testament to the language of the people, a process that continues today. No matter what language someone speaks, God's Word can still proclaim freedom in Christ to them.

4   THE FORMULA OF CONCORD

After Luther died, his German followers argued about what his teachings really meant. For the next 30 years, they fought about how God's law works, whether we have free will, and what happens in the Lord's Supper. They managed to settle these issues and published their agreement: The Formula of Concord. Along with the Augsburg Confession, the Formula of Concord helps the church's preachers and teachers know how to do their work so people can hear what Christ has done for them.

5 SERMONS

Perhaps the most important work the Lutheran reformers did was to change what pastors preached. Martin Luther argued that God's Word had been held captive by bad preaching. By changing preaching to focus on proclaiming the gospel, Luther and the other reformers hoped to make sure God's promises could be freed to inspire people of faith. When that happened, people could actually trust Jesus as their Savior.

Martin Luther nailed his Ninety-five Theses to a church door in Wittenberg, setting the Reformation in motion. One of Luther's main attacks was against the sale of "indulgences," which claimed that people could buy their way into heaven.

FIVE COMMON WORSHIP PRACTICES AND WHY LUTHERANS DO THEM

While some language and gestures during Lutheran worship can seem bizarre to the uninitiated, they do not indicate cultism. There is a solid, biblical reason for each one and knowing the reason can add meaning and satisfaction to your worship experience.

1 PASSING THE PEACE

It might seem like your weekly chance to say hello to everyone, but passing the peace is more than hand shaking and small talk. "Peace be with you" was the greeting of the risen Christ to his disciples (see John 20:19) and sharing the peace extends Jesus' blessing. The practice grew out of the "kiss of peace" (see Romans 16:16), an ancient ritual symbolizing one's close relationship to another person.

2 TAKING AN OFFERING

Lutherans collect an offering as a tangible response to God's blessings to us. God's people for centuries have been challenged to return a tenth of their possessions (a "tithe") to the service of the Lord. An offering goes far beyond money and includes our time, energy, talents, and the use of our material possessions. We are called to offer *everything* that we have to God. But the money's pretty important.

3 SAYING, "AND ALSO WITH YOU"

The congregation generally provides this response after the worship leader gives a blessing (such as "The Lord be with you") before a prayer. To respond, "And also with you," returns the blessing to the leader, giving the message, "We're in this together."

A key way Lutherans participate actively in the worship service is by singing songs and hymns. This is an old tradition, and it still works.

4 SINGING HYMNS

For much of history, worshipers participated by simply watching leaders preach, pray, sing, and celebrate Holy Communion. Martin Luther sought to broaden participation through an important component: the singing of hymns. Hymns often express the themes explored elsewhere in worship, such as in the Bible readings, sermon, or Holy Communion, while inviting the whole congregation to participate.

5 RECEIVING THE BENEDICTION

A benediction is a blessing (*bene* = good, *dictio* = to say). It marks the close of the worship service and our return into the world, a reminder of God's grace and presence as we go. While there are variations, a common benediction is, "Almighty God, Father, Son, and Holy Spirit, bless you now and forever." Also common is the Aaronic Benediction, which begins: "The Lord bless you and keep you"—the blessing that Aaron gave to his fellow Israelites (see Numbers 6:22-27).

FIVE FACTS ABOUT LIFE IN MEDIEVAL TIMES

1   IT LASTED MORE THAN 1,000 YEARS.
By some counts, the medieval period (or Middle Ages) covered an era that began around the year 391 (when Christianity became the Roman Empire's only legal religion) and ended around 1517 (the year Martin Luther wrote the Ninety-five Theses).

2   LIFE WAS NASTY, BRUTISH, AND SHORT.
People who survived childhood usually did not live long past age 40. If disease or starvation didn't get you, violence and warfare did. It's been estimated that during the 1400s about one-third of Europe's population died of bubonic plague. Sanitation was practically non-existent.

Road travel was harsh and sanitation was minimal during the Middle Ages.

3 THE CHRISTIAN CHURCH GREW LARGER, MORE INFLUENTIAL, AND MORE DOMINANT.

Headquartered in Rome, the Western church became a super-power. Church and state became inseparable. At its height (ca. 1000–1300), "Christian Crusaders" battled with Muslims and others for control of the "Holy Land," Thomas Aquinas wrote his *Summa Theologica*, and hundreds of "heretics" were burned to death.

4 THE "CULT OF THE SAINTS" DEVELOPED.

Over the centuries, a system grew in which the leftover good works (merits) of the saints could be distributed to others, with the pope in charge of this store (treasury) of good works. With his Ninety-five Theses, Luther challenged this system.

5 HUMANIST AND RENAISSANCE-AGE THINKERS ALSO WORKED FOR REFORM.

At the end of the Middle Ages, early reformers such as Jan Hus and Girolamo Savonarola confronted the church corruptions they saw. Hus was burned, and Savonarola was hanged. For other examples, see "History's Six Most Notorious Heretics" on the next two pages.

HISTORY'S SIX MOST NOTORIOUS HERETICS

Though vilified by those who write history, heretics played a critical role in the church. They refined its message and forced the church to be honest with itself. But heretics usually payed the ultimate price, and often they were wrong.

1 **HYPATIA OF ALEXANDRIA (370–415)**
Hypatia was an African philosopher, mathematician, physicist, astronomer, and director of Alexandria's Library, once the largest in the world. Bishop Cyril of Alexandria, out of jealousy, declared her a heretic and ordered her to be tortured and burned at the stake, together with her writings. Her mistakes were to prefer study to marriage, to know more than the bishop, and to be a female teacher of males.

2 **PELAGIUS (354–418)**
Pelagius was a Celtic monk who believed in the goodness of human nature and the freedom of human will. These beliefs led him to denounce the doctrine of original sin—a core tenet of the church—and suggest that human beings were equal participants in their salvation with Jesus Christ. The *Pelagianism* movement, named after him, was a strict teaching of self-reliance. When Pelagius taught that one could achieve grace without the church, he was excommunicated.

3 **JOAN OF ARC (1412–1431)**
Joan was a French peasant girl who was able to hear heavenly voices that urged her to liberate her nation from the British occupation. She was 19 when sentenced as a heretic and burned at the stake. Joan's fault was to be a better army leader than men. She is now a national hero.

4 GIROLAMO SAVONAROLA (1452–1498)

His parents wanted him to be a physician, but this Italian youngster decided to be a Dominican monk and serve people who were poor. He preached against Pope Alexander VI and the powerful Medici family. Members of the wealthy church and society hung and burned him, then threw his ashes in the Arnos River to prevent him from having a restful place.

5 MARTIN LUTHER (1483–1546)

His father, a peasant and coal miner, wanted him to be a lawyer. Martin disappointed him and became an Augustinian monk. Emperor Charles V and Pope Leo X threw him out of the church and put a price on his head, but Luther continued serving the poor, preaching and living the Bible, and sharing hospitality at the family dinner table.

6 HATUEY (?–1511)

This Native American leader from the Guahaba region escaped from Haiti to Cuba. The brave Hatuey was captured and declared a heretic. A priest wanted to baptize him in order for the Indian to get to heaven after being burnt. The Ta'no chief rejected the Christian rite when he heard that in heaven there would also be people from Spain.

CHURCH STUFF

COMPARATIVE RELIGIONS

	Baha'i	Buddhism	Christianity
Founder and date founded	Bahá'u'lláh (1817-1892) founded Babism in 1844 from which Baha'i grew.	Founded by Siddhartha Gautama (the Buddha) in Nepal in the 6th-5th centuries B.C.E.	Founded by Jesus of Nazareth, a Palestinian Jew, in the early 1st century C.E.
Number of adherents in 2000	About 7 million worldwide; 750,000 U.S.	360 million worldwide; 2 million U.S.	About 2 billion worldwide; 160 million U.S.
Main tenets	The oneness of God, the oneness of humanity, and the common foundation of all religion. Also, equality of men and women, universal education, world peace, and a world federal government.	Meditation and the practice of virtuous and moral behavior can lead to Nirvana, the state of enlightenment. Before that, one is subjected to repeated lifetimes, based on behavior.	Jesus is the Son of God and God in human form. In his death and resurrection, he redeems humanity from sin and gives believers eternal life. His teachings frame the godly life for his followers.
Sacred or primary writing	Bahá'u'lláh's teachings, along with those of the Bab, are collected and published.	The Buddha's teachings and wisdom are collected and published.	The Bible is a collection of Jewish and Near Eastern writings spanning some 1,400 years.

Confucianism	Hinduism	Islam	Judaism
Founded by the Chinese philosopher Confucius in the 6th-5th centuries B.C.E. One of several traditional Chinese religions.	Developed in the 2nd century B.C.E. from indigenous religions in India, and later combined with other religions, such as Vaishnavism.	Founded by the prophet Muhammad ca. C.E. 610. The word Islam is Arabic for "submission to God."	Founded by Abraham, Isaac, and Jacob ca. 2000 B.C.E.
6 million worldwide (does not include other traditional Chinese beliefs); U.S. uncertain.	900 million worldwide; 950,000 U.S.	1.3 billion worldwide; 5.6 million U.S.	14 million worldwide; 5.5 million U.S.
Confucius's followers wrote down his sayings or Analects. They stress relationships between individuals, families, and society based on proper behavior and sympathy.	Hinduism is based on a broad system of sects. The goal is release from repeated reincarnation through yoga, adherence to the Vedic scriptures, and devotion to a personal guru.	Followers worship Allah through the Five Pillars. Muslims who die believing in God, and that Muhammad is God's messenger, will enter Paradise.	Judaism holds the belief in a monotheistic God, whose Word is revealed in the Hebrew Bible, especially the Torah. Jews await the coming of a messiah to restore creation.
Confucius's Analects are collected and still published.	The Hindu scriptures and Vedic texts.	The Koran is a collection of Muhammad's writings.	The Hebrew scriptures compose the Christian Old Testament.

WORLD RELIGIONS

Listed by approximate number of adherents:

Christianity	2 billion
Islam	1.3 billion
Hinduism	900 million
Agnostic/Atheist/Non-Religious	850 million
Buddhism	360 million
Confucianism and Chinese traditional	225 million
Primal-indigenous	150 million
Shinto	108 million
African traditional	95 million
Sikhism	23 million
Juche	19 million
Judaism	14 million
Spiritism	14 million
Baha'i	7 million
Jainism	4 million
Cao Dai	3 million
Tenrikyo	2.4 million
Neo-Paganism	1 million
Unitarian-Universalism	800,000
Rastafarianism	700,000
Scientology	600,000
Zoroastrianism	150,000

FAMILY TREE
OF CHRISTIANITY

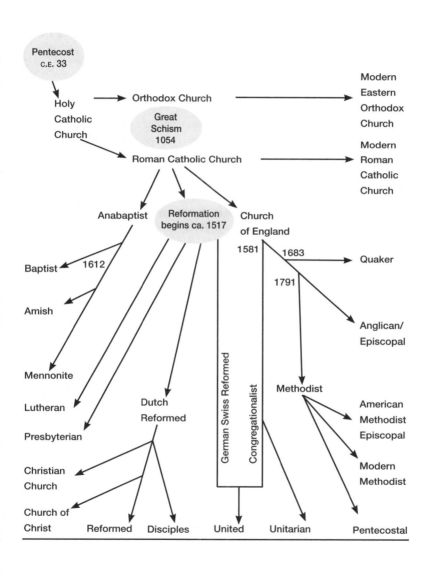

COMPARATIVE DENOMINATIONS:

	Lutheran	Catholic	Orthodox
Founded when and by whom?	1517: Martin Luther challenges Catholic teachings with his Ninety-five Theses. 1530: the Augsburg Confession is published.	Catholics consider Jesus' disciple Peter (died ca. C.E. 66) the first pope. Through Gregory the Great (540–604), papacy is firmly established.	C.E 330: Emperor Constantine renames Byzantium "Constantinople" and declares Christianity the empire's religion.
Adherents in 2000?	About 60 million worldwide; about 9 million U.S.	About 1 billion worldwide; 60 million U.S.	About 225 million worldwide; about 4 million U.S.
How is Scripture viewed?	Protestant canon contains 39 OT books, 27 NT. Scripture alone is the authoritative witness to the gospel.	The canon is 46 books in the OT (Apocryhpha included) and 27 in the NT. Interpretation is subject to church tradition.	49 OT books (Catholic plus three more) and 27 NT. Scripture is subject to tradition.
How are we saved?	We are saved by grace when God grants righteousness through faith alone. Good works inevitably result, but they are not the basis of salvation.	God infuses the gift of faith in the baptized, which is maintained by good works and receiving Penance and the Eucharist.	God became human so humans could be deified, that is, have the energy of God's life in them.
What is the church?	The congregation of believers, mixed with the lost, in which the gospel is preached and the sacraments are administered.	The mystical body of Christ, who established it with the pope as its head; he pronounces doctrine infallibly.	The body of Christ in unbroken historical connection with the apostles; the Roman pope is one of many patriarchs who govern.
What about the sacraments?	Baptism is necessary for salvation. The Lord's Supper is bread & wine that, with God's Word, are truly Jesus' body and blood.	Catholics hold seven sacraments. Baptism removes original sin; usually infants. The Eucharist undergoes transubstantiation.	Baptism initiates God's life in the baptized; adults and children. In the Eucharist, bread & wine are changed into body and blood.

LITURGICAL CHURCHES

	Anglican	Presbyterian	Methodist
Founded when and by whom?	1534: Henry VIII is declared head of the Church of England. 1549: Thomas Cranmer produces the first Book of Common Prayer.	1536: John Calvin writes Institutes of the Christian Religion. 1789: Presbyterian Church U.S.A. is organized.	1738: Anglican ministers John and Charles Wesley convert. 1784: U.S. Methodists form a separate church body.
Adherents in 2000?	45-75 million worldwide; about 3 million U.S.	40-48 million worldwide; 4 million U.S.	20-40 million worldwide; about 13 million U.S.
How is Scripture viewed?	Protestant canon accepted. Scripture is interpreted in light of tradition and reason.	Protestant canon accepted. Scripture is "witness without parallel" to Christ, but in human words reflecting beliefs of the time.	Protestant canon accepted. Scripture is primary source for Christian doctrine.
How are we saved?	We share in Christ's victory, who died for our sins, freeing us through baptism to become living members of the church.	We are saved by grace alone. Good works result, but are not the basis of salvation.	We are saved by grace alone. Good works must result, but do not obtain salvation.
What is the church?	The body of Christ is based on "apostolic succession" of bishops, going back to the apostles. In the U.S., it is the Episcopal Church.	The body of Christ includes all of God's chosen and is represented by the visible church. Governed by regional "presbyteries" of elders.	The body of Christ, represented by church institutions. Bishops oversee regions and appoint pastors, who are itinerant.
What about the sacraments?	Baptism brings infant and convert initiates into the church; in Communion, Christ's body and blood are truly present.	Baptism is not necessary for salvation. The Lord's Supper is Christ's body and blood, which are spiritually present to believers.	Baptism is a sign of regeneration; in the Lord's Supper, Jesus is really present.

THE SEASONS
OF THE CHURCH YEAR
AND WHAT THEY MEAN

ADVENT is a season of longing and anticipation, during which we prepare for the coming of Jesus. The church year begins with Advent, as life begins with birth, starting four Sundays before Christmas. The liturgical color for Advent is blue, which symbolizes waiting and hope.

CHRISTMAS is a day and a season when we celebrate God's coming among us as a human child: Jesus, Emmanuel (which means "God with us"). The liturgical color for Christmas is white, which reminds us that Jesus is the Light of the world. Christmas lasts for 12 days, from December 25 to January 5.

EPIPHANY is celebrated on January 6, when we remember the three Wise Men's visit to the Christ child. The color for Epiphany Day is white. During the time after Epiphany we hear stories about Jesus' baptism and early ministry. The color for these Sundays is sometimes white and sometimes green. On the last Sunday we celebrate the Transfiguration. The color for this day is white, and we hear the story of Jesus shining brightly on the mountaintop.

LENT is a season when we turn toward God and think about how our lives need to change. This is also a time to remember our baptism, and how that gift gives us a new start every day! The color for Lent is purple, symbolizing repentance. Lent begins on Ash Wednesday and lasts for 40 days (not including Sundays) and ends on the Saturday before Easter Sunday.

THE THREE DAYS are the most important part of the Christian calendar because they mark Jesus' last days, death, and resurrection. These days (approximately three 24-hour periods) begin on Maundy Thursday evening and conclude on Easter evening. On Maundy Thursday we hear the story of Jesus' last meal with his disciples and his act of service and love in washing their feet. On Good Friday we hear of Jesus' trial, crucifixion, death, and burial. On Saturday, at the nighttime Easter Vigil, we hear stories about the amazing things God has done for us. It is a night of light, Scripture readings, baptismal remembrance, and communion—the greatest night of the year for Christians. On Easter Sunday we celebrate Jesus' resurrection and our new lives in Christ. Easter falls on a different date each year—sometime between March 22 and April 25.

EASTER is not just one day, but a whole season when we celebrate the resurrected Jesus. The season begins on Easter Sunday and lasts for 50 days (including Sundays). The color is white, symbolizing resurrection and joy. The Day of Pentecost falls on the 50th day of the season (Pentecost means 50th), when we honor the Holy Spirit and the church's mission in the world. This day uses the fiery color of red.

TIME AFTER PENTECOST is the longest season in the church calendar, lasting almost half the year. Sometimes this is called "ordinary time" because there aren't many special celebrations during these weeks. The liturgical color for the time after Pentecost is green, representing life and growth. Each week we hear a different story about Jesus' ministry from one of the four Gospels.

SPECIAL FESTIVALS are celebrated throughout the year. Some festivals occur the same time every year, such as Reformation Sunday (last Sunday in October) and All Saints Sunday (first Sunday in November). Others, like saints' days, we might celebrate only when their day falls on a Sunday. The color for these days is either white or red.

THE SEASONS
OF THE CHURCH YEAR

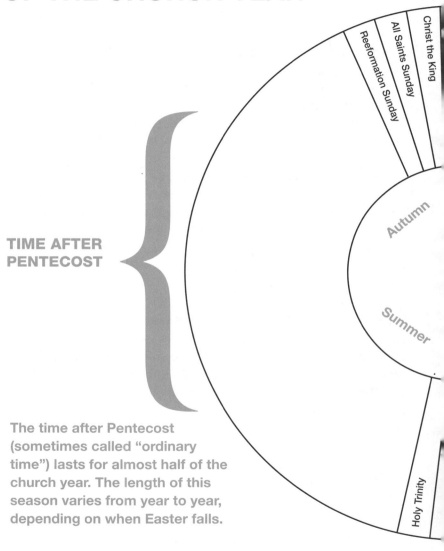

**TIME AFTER
PENTECOST**

The time after Pentecost
(sometimes called "ordinary
time") lasts for almost half of the
church year. The length of this
season varies from year to year,
depending on when Easter falls.

Christ the King

All Saints Sunday

Reformation Sunday

Autumn

Summer

Holy Trinity

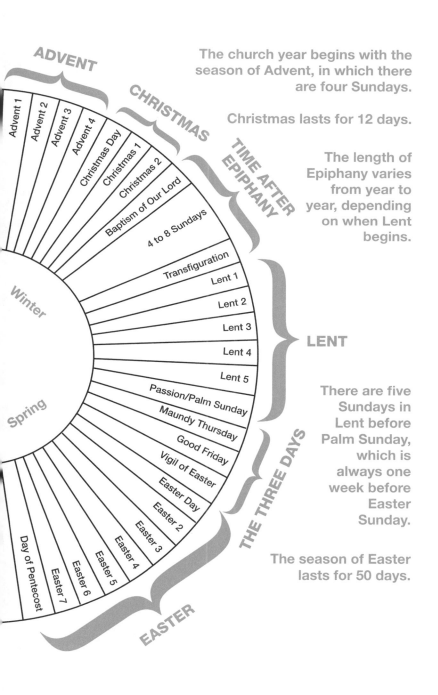

ADVENT

CHRISTMAS

Advent 1
Advent 2
Advent 3
Advent 4
Christmas Day
Christmas 1
Christmas 2
Baptism of Our Lord

TIME AFTER EPIPHANY

4 to 8 Sundays

Transfiguration

Lent 1
Lent 2
Lent 3
Lent 4
Lent 5

Passion/Palm Sunday
Maundy Thursday
Good Friday
Vigil of Easter
Easter Day
Easter 2
Easter 3
Easter 4
Easter 5
Easter 6
Easter 7
Day of Pentecost

Winter

Spring

THE THREE DAYS

EASTER

The church year begins with the season of Advent, in which there are four Sundays.

Christmas lasts for 12 days.

The length of Epiphany varies from year to year, depending on when Lent begins.

LENT

There are five Sundays in Lent before Palm Sunday, which is always one week before Easter Sunday.

The season of Easter lasts for 50 days.

EVERYDAY STUFF

Believing in God involves more than going to church and reading the Bible. It's about keeping your faith with you in every part of your life.

This section includes:

] Advice for helping people in times of trouble.

] Tips on forgiving others and treating them with respect—even if you don't always feel like it.

] Suggestions for avoiding temptation on a daily basis. Some of these ideas go back to the Middle Ages.

HOW TO TELL THE DIFFERENCE BETWEEN THE LAW AND THE GOSPEL

Discerning law from gospel is a critical skill for Christians and the hallmark of Lutheranism. Law and gospel are always connected to God's word. God brings them to you in the Bible, in preaching, in the sacraments, and in all kinds of daily activity. If you listen closely, you'll hear God speaking both law and gospel.

THE LAW

Martin Luther suggested that the law has two uses: First, to point out and condemn sin. Second, to drive the sinner toward the grace and mercy revealed in Jesus Christ and his cross.

1 **LISTEN FOR THE "SHOULD."**
God uses the law to tell us what we ought to do so we maintain an orderly, peaceful, and secure world. It therefore always sounds like a demand. Words such as *should*, *ought to*, *must, have to*, and *shall* are a dead giveaway that the law is around somewhere.

2 **LISTEN FOR THE FIRST COMMANDMENT.**
"You shall have no other gods," is what all other law rises from. The law's goal is to force sinners to act as though God's will is more important than our own.

3 **DISCERN WHO'S IN CHARGE.**
Demands always require you to do something to fulfill them. If you're being urged to act a certain way to make something happen, it's the law talking.

4 BE ALERT TO DEATH LURKING IN THE SHADOWS.
When you feel like the demands of life are just about killing you, you can be pretty sure it's God's law nipping at your heels.

THE GOSPEL

1 LISTEN FOR THE PROMISE.
If what you're hearing tells you what Christ promises you—without any action on your part—then the gospel is present.

2 EXPECT A RADICAL SURPRISE FROM JESUS.
We sinners should never expect the good news; we should only expect God's judgment. Instead, the gospel brings sinners mercy and life from Jesus.

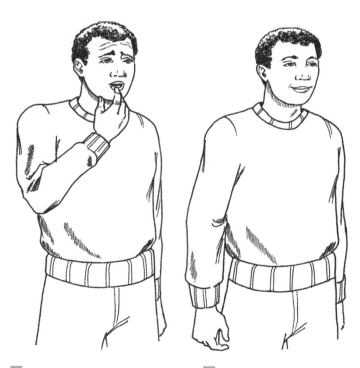

The law accuses and demands.

The gospel liberates and frees us.

EVERYDAY STUFF

3 LISTEN FOR THE "FOR YOU."

The gospel is always spoken directly to sinners. If what you hear doesn't use the word *you*, it could be a good description about God or Jesus, but it's not quite the gospel. The gospel says it straight out: "You are forgiven." "Jesus died for you."

4 REMEMBER THE PROMISE.

When God's word has changed you, you'll see God's faithfulness in spite of the injustice in the world. When it has caused you to trust God, even though the world says you're a loser, then you can be sure you've heard the gospel.

BE AWARE

] Law and gospel can't be defined strictly. They are the *ways* we experience the following two things:

1. God is working continually to confront and put to death the "you" that turns away and puts your trust in other things. When the law does its work, that's what God is doing.

2. God is also working continually to create a new faithful person in you. When the gospel does its work, that's what God is doing.

] God sometimes does only the first thing, but God never brings the gospel without the law being present first. It's only when the law stops us from thinking we can make life work out on our own that we become open to hearing God's promises.

HOW TO SHARE YOUR FAITH WITH SOMEONE

Sharing the gospel with others is a natural part of exercising a mature faith. In fact, Jesus commanded his followers to do this, making it an important part of the life of faith (Matthew 28:18-20). Still, Lutherans tend to be rather shy evangelists.

While *evangelism* has become a negative word for some people, sharing the story of salvation in Jesus Christ is still the most rewarding way to live out one's faith. It is also a discipline that takes practice.

1 **LOOK FOR THE OPENING.**
    Regular daily conversations offer lots of chances to talk about your faith. Listen for open-ended comments, such as, "I wonder why life is like that," or, "Sometimes life seems so hard." When possible, offer a response from a Christian perspective. Begin sentences with phrases such as, "I've come to think . . ." or, "I don't have the perfect answer, but I believe . . ."

2 **BE YOURSELF.**
    Expressing your faith should be natural and the same as other types of daily conversation. Avoid suddenly switching your tone of voice or vocabulary. Also, don't try to impress the other person with your knowledge. Allow the Holy Spirit to guide you.

EVERYDAY STUFF

3 WATCH FOR A CHANCE TO TAKE THE CONVERSATION DEEPER.

Carefully gauge the other person's response. Observe his or her facial expression, verbal tone, and body language. If he or she seems to be closing down, set the topic aside and wait for another time. If he or she keys in and perks up, be prepared to continue.

4 OPEN UP.

Human beings are attracted to each other by our strengths, but we bond because of our weaknesses. Key to sharing your faith is the willingness to be honest about your own life's struggles. This will communicate safety, which for many people is critical.

5 FOLLOW UP.

Offer to continue the conversation later and arrange a time. At this point, the conversation will have become personally valuable to you. Allowing the person to see your commitment to your faith alongside your continuing questions will reassure him or her of your sincerity.

6 OFFER TO SHARE YOUR FAITH COMMUNITY WITH THE OTHER PERSON.

Most people join a church after being invited by a friend. When the time is right, invite the person to attend with you. Tell the person what makes it special to you.

7 TRY TO MAINTAIN THE RELATIONSHIP REGARDLESS OF WHAT THE PERSON DOES.

Be prepared for the other person to shut down around faith talk, decline your invitation to attend church, or even appear to avoid you. The most effective way to communicate that you're a follower of Jesus Christ is through your actions; continue to live naturally and with integrity. Watch for another opportunity to open the subject later on.

HOW TO PRAY

Prayer is intimate communication with God and can be used before a meal, at bedtime, during a worship service, or any time the need or opportunity arises. Silent and spoken prayers are both okay and may be used liberally throughout the day. Prayer is also taking time to listen to what God is saying to us. Spontaneous prayer is often best, but the following process may help build the habit.

1 **ASSESS YOUR NEED FOR PRAYER.**
Take stock of the situation at hand, including your motivations. What are you praying *for* and why?

2 **SELECT A TYPE OF PRAYER.**
Prayers of *supplication* (requests for God's help), *contrition* (in which sin is confessed and forgiveness requested), *intercession* (on behalf of others), and others are good and time tested. Books of personal prayers, hymnals, and devotionals often contain helpful, prewritten prayers. Consider also an ad-libbed prayer from the heart.

3 **SELECT A PHYSICAL PRAYER POSTURE.**
Many postures are appropriate:

- The most common type of prayer in the New Testament is from a prone position, lying face-down on the ground, arms spread.

- Kneeling with your face and palms upturned is good for prayers of supplication.

- Bowed head with closed eyes and hands folded is common today and aids concentration.

There is no "official" posture for prayer. Choose your posture according to your individual prayer needs.

I Choose a comfortable and appropriate prayer posture for your prayer time.

4 OFFER YOUR PRAYER.
Pray with confidence. God listens to all prayer and responds. Breathe deeply, relax, and be open as the Spirit leads you.

5 LISTEN.
Take time during your prayer simply to listen. Some prayer traditions involve only silent meditation as a means of listening for God's voice.

BE AWARE

] God hears every prayer.

] Prayer can be done either alone or in the company of others (corporately).

] Environment matters. If possible, consider lighting a candle and dimming the lights to set the correct mood and help block out distractions.

HOW TO WORK FOR PEACE AND JUSTICE ON BEHALF OF PEOPLE WHO ARE POOR AND OPPRESSED

Knowing that good works are the result—not the cause—of salvation, Lutherans have a long and extraordinary record of working for economic justice and relief around the world. Lutheran World Relief, for example, ranks among the world's most powerful aid organizations, often responding faster, longer, and with larger resources than other groups.

Lutheran congregations around the globe also set justice as one of their highest priorities, giving time and money both locally and globally. As followers of Jesus Christ, each individual Christian is linked to Jesus' compassion for people who are poor and called to work tirelessly on their behalf, as he did.

1 **INCLUDE PEOPLE WHO ARE POOR AND OPPRESSED IN YOUR DAILY PRAYERS.**
Keeping the needs of others in mind, especially people who suffer as a result of economic inequality, political oppression, or natural disaster, defines a person's good works. Name specific situations in your prayers, and use specific place names and people's names whenever possible. Keep the newspaper on your lap as you pray, if necessary.

2 **INCLUDE PEOPLE WHO ARE POOR AND OPPRESSED IN YOUR PERSONAL OR HOUSEHOLD BUDGET.**
Dedicate some of your personal giving to economic-aid organizations. This should include your congregation. If you already tithe (give 10 percent of your income to your church), consider earmarking a percentage of that money to go directly to relief organizations through your church's budget.

3 **PAY CLOSE ATTENTION TO ECONOMIC AND POLITICAL CONDITIONS IN OTHER NATIONS.**
You can't help if you don't know what's really going on. Resolve to be a well-informed person who tests the worldview in the news against the worldview in the Bible. Utilize the Internet to locate independent and alternative news sources with unique, on-the-spot perspectives.

4 **GET TO KNOW ORGANIZATIONS THAT WORK FOR JUSTICE LOCALLY.**
Your congregation probably already organizes to do justice work in your neighborhood. If not, consider taking responsibility to organize a ministry team in your church.

5 **MAKE WORKING FOR JUSTICE PART OF YOUR WEEKLY OR MONTHLY ROUTINE.**
Devote a portion of your time regularly to a specific activity that personally connects you to people who are poor and disenfranchised. There is no substitute for personal contact.

6 **VOTE YOUR CONSCIENCE.**
  If you are of voting age, remember that nations will be judged by the way they treat people who are disadvantaged. Keep this in mind when you go to your polling place.

7 **ADVOCATE FOR A CAUSE IN WHICH YOU BELIEVE, ONE THAT HAS MEANING FOR YOU PERSONALLY.**

HOW TO IDENTIFY A GENUINE MIRACLE

The term *miracle* describes something that causes wonder. It is usually used in reference to an event that defies logical explanation and appears to be the work of a higher force, suggesting a reality beyond the five senses.

1 DISREGARD MOST MINOR SITUATIONS.
The facts should indicate a situation of high order, such as one that is life threatening, one involving suffering, or involving an immediate threat. Finding your lost keys does not necessarily constitute a miracle.

2 LOOK FOR A LACK OF PREDICTABILITY.
A positive outcome should be needed and wanted, but not expected. Miracles tend to occur "out of the blue" rather than as the result of an earthly cause, especially a human one.

3 EVALUATE THE OUTCOME.
Miracles achieve a life-giving purpose; they never occur outside the will of God. Suffering is relieved, God is glorified, Jesus' presence is made manifest, the lowly are lifted up, evil is thwarted, creation is revealed, or life is saved. The outcome *must* be regarded as good, according to biblical standards.

4 LOOK FOR A DIVINE AGENCY.

The ability to make a miracle happen, to guarantee the results, or to take credit for it is beyond human. Often, the event will defy what we know to be true about the laws of nature or probability. If anyone stands to make money or advance an agenda from an event, it is most likely not a miracle.

5 ADOPT A WAIT-AND-SEE PERSPECTIVE.

A miracle will still be a miracle later on. Labeling something a miracle too quickly could lead down unhelpful paths, while waiting to make the call—pondering the event in your heart—will enhance your faith journey.

BE AWARE

]   The most overlooked miracle is that God shows up in everyday life events and in such ordinary forms as bread, wine, water, words, and people.

]   The miracle of life in Jesus Christ is a daily event and should be regarded as a free gift.

THREE ESSENTIAL PERSONAL SPIRITUAL RITUALS

A spiritual ritual is a routine for building one's faith. Ritual involves action, words, and often images that work together to center one's daily life in Jesus Christ. Medical studies show that people who pray regularly throughout the day suffer less stress, have lower incidence of heart disease, and live longer on average than those who do not.

1 MORNING DEVOTIONS

- Directly upon awakening, turn your attention first to God. The silence and solitude available in the morning hours are ideal. (See Luther's Morning Blessing on page 309.)

- Try to make prayer the first activity of your day. If necessary, set your alarm to sound 15 minutes early to give yourself time.

- Begin with thanks and by remembering God's constant presence.

- Identify events you anticipate in your day and how you feel about them.

- Ask God to provide what you need for the day.

- Pray on behalf of other people. Consider keeping a list of names tucked inside your Bible or devotional book.

2 MEALTIME GRACE

Human beings naturally pause before a meal. Use those moments to give thanks.

- Consider establishing mealtime grace as a household ritual.

- When eating in public, be considerate of others, but do not abandon your ritual.

- Once your meal is assembled and ready to eat, take time before praying to gather your thoughts and call an appropriate prayer to mind.

Praying before mealtime is a great personal ritual that can be shared with others.

- Many people pray a rote or memorized prayer at mealtimes. Consider occasionally departing from your regular prayer with an extemporaneous one.

3 EVENING PRAYER

The other daily rituals you perform in the evening, like brushing your teeth or letting the cat out, create a natural structure for evening prayer.

- Establish a regular time, such as sunset or at bedtime, and commit to it.

- Confess wrongdoing and ask for forgiveness.

- Tell God about the joys and sorrows of the day. Ask for help with the sorrows and give thanks for the joys.

- Identify the good things about the day. On bad days, find at least one thing to give thanks for.

- Consider using a devotional as a guide and companion. (See Luther's Evening Blessing on page 310.)

- Think about involving other members of your household in this ritual. Evening prayer particularly can be enhanced through sharing. When children are included, trace the cross on their foreheads and say a brief blessing as part of the ritual. (See illustration on page 219.)

HOW TO FORGIVE SOMEONE

Forgiving is one of the most difficult disciplines of faith, since it seems to cost you something additional when you've already been wronged. Swallowing your pride and seeking a greater good, however, can yield great healing and growth.

1 ACKNOWLEDGE THAT GOD FORGIVES YOU.
When you realize that God has already shown forgiveness, and continues to forgive sinners like you, it's easier to forgive someone else.

2 CONSULT SCRIPTURE.
Jesus taught the Lord's Prayer to his disciples, who were hungry to become like he was. Forgiveness was a big part of this. Read Matthew 6:9-15.

3 SEEK THE PERSON OUT WHENEVER POSSIBLE.
Consciously decide to deliver your forgiveness in person. In cases where this is geographically impossible, find an appropriate alternative means, such as the telephone.

Note: This may not be wise in all cases, given the timing of the situation or the level of hurt. Certain problems can be made worse by an unwelcome declaration of forgiveness. Consult with a clergyperson before taking questionable action.

4 SAY, "I FORGIVE YOU," OUT LOUD.
A verbal declaration of forgiveness is ideal. Speaking the words enacts a physical chain reaction that can create healing for both speaker and hearer. In the Bible, Jesus used these words to heal a paralyzed man from across a room.

EVERYDAY STUFF

5   PRAY FOR THE POWER TO FORGIVE.

Praying for this is always good, whether a forgiveness situation is at hand or not. It is especially helpful in cases where declaring forgiveness seems beyond your reach.

BE AWARE

] When someone sins against you personally, forgiving them does NOT depend upon them feeling sorry (showing contrition) or asking for your forgiveness. But it helps. You may have to struggle, however, to forgive them without their consent or participation.

HOW TO CONFESS YOUR SINS AND RECEIVE FORGIVENESS

Confession is an "office of the keys" belonging to all baptized persons, that is, anyone may confess and any believer may pronounce the word of forgiveness. A declaration of forgiveness is permanent and binding because it comes from Jesus Christ himself.

1   **MAKE A MENTAL LIST OF YOUR OFFENSES.**

2   **LOCATE A FELLOW CHRISTIAN.**
    When appropriate, confess your sins to another person.

3   **RESOLVE TO CONFESS OF YOUR OWN FREE WILL.**
    Don't confess merely because someone else wants you to do it. Make your confession voluntarily.

4   **MAKE YOUR CONFESSION FEARLESSLY, ALOUD IF POSSIBLE.**
    Confess the sins that burden you, and then confess the sins of which you are not aware or can't remember.

5   **AVOID MAKING UP SINS.**
    More important than the facts and figures is a spirit of repentance in your heart.

6   **RECEIVE FORGIVENESS AS IT IS GIVEN, IN THE NAME OF THE FATHER AND OF THE SON AND OF THE HOLY SPIRIT.**
    God forgives you fully. Make the sign of the cross to help you remember.

7   **RESOLVE TO LIVE JOYFULLY AND PENITENTLY.**
    With absolution comes new life in the freedom of God's grace.

BE AWARE

] Unburdening your conscience through confession is cleansing and good for the soul; it's not meant to be torture.

] Ultimately, forgiveness comes from God. A perfect and pure confession is not a strict requirement to receive it.

HOW TO MAKE THE SIGN OF THE CROSS

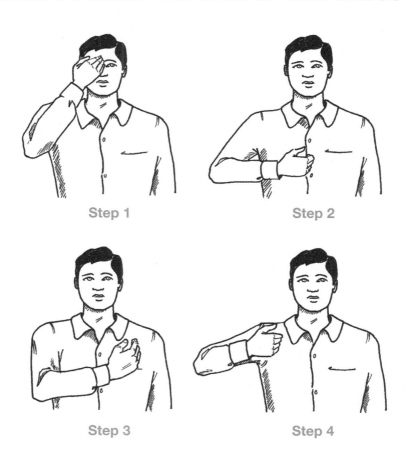

Step 1   Step 2

Step 3   Step 4

HOW TO DEFEND YOUR FAITH AGAINST ATTACK

Defending your faith from attack involves tact and savvy, that is, the ability to empathize with your adversary and use his or her affronts creatively without getting baited into an angry or hostile response. The Lutheran theological perspective was hammered out in a context of debate and controversy, though you probably don't need to go looking for a fight nowadays. Just be ready. There is no substitute for knowing your stuff.

1 **EMPLOY THE 80/20 RULE.**
   In any debate, it is best to listen at least 80 percent of the time and talk 20 percent of the time.

2 **ENGAGE IN EMPATHIC LISTENING.**
   Empathic listening means to try to comprehend not just the content of the other person's position, but also the emotional thrust behind it. This is important especially in cases where the speaker's emotional expressions are intense.

3 **RESTATE YOUR ADVERSARY'S ARGUMENT EMPATHETICALLY.**
   Use sentences like, "So, you're upset because Christians seem to say one thing and do another."

4 **IDENTIFY WITH WHAT THE SPEAKER IS SAYING.**
   For example, say, "I know what you mean. I see a lot of phony behavior at my own church." This elevates the conversation and keeps it civil.

EVERYDAY STUFF

5 **DO YOUR BEST TO PUT THE SPEAKER AT EASE.**
Having made clear that you understand his or her position, you are free to state your defense or counterpoint. Offer "I statement" responses, such as, "I wonder how I would stand up under that kind of scrutiny, myself," or, "I do my best not to judge others too harshly. I'd hate to be judged by those standards."

6 **KEEP IT AS UPBEAT AS POSSIBLE.**
Use humility, humor, and a pleasant nature to defuse any tension. Though hard to practice, it is possible to disagree with someone while remaining friends.

7 **GIVE YOUR OPPONENT HIS OR HER DUE.**
When the speaker makes a good argument, say, "You make a good point." This will further elevate the conversation. If you still disagree, make your counterargument calmly.

8 **AVOID CLOSING OFF THE CONVERSATION OR LEAVING IT ON A SOUR NOTE.**
If you can, offer to continue the discussion over a lunch that you buy. Avoid falling into a "winner take all" mind-set. Keep respect as your highest value.

BE AWARE

] Attacks on faith are not limited to verbal assaults, especially in countries such as China or Vietnam, where religious persecution is a reality. Take care when visiting such places, especially when distributing religious materials or sharing stories about your faith.

] It is best in all cases to avoid sounding smug or preachy where your points resemble counterattacks.

HOW TO RESIST TEMPTATION

Lutherans have inherited lots of good advice from Martin Luther. One thing we've lost is the down-to-earth, common sense ways that Luther advised people to resist temptation. These are ideas he gave people who said they were tempted.

1 **RUN THE OPPOSITE DIRECTION.**
   Learn to identify the things that tempt you and avoid situations in which temptation will occur. When you see a temptation coming down the road, take a detour.

2 **LAUGH AT THE TEMPTER.**
   Temptations are simply things that want to gain power over you. When you laugh at them, you reduce them to their proper place.

3 **DISTRACT YOURSELF WITH OTHER, HEALTHIER ACTIVITIES.**
   God knows what's good for you and so do you. Find an alternate activity that promotes trust in God and requires you to care for your neighbors. Seek the company of others, especially people to whom you may be of service.

4 **REMEMBER, YOUR LORD ALSO CONFRONTED TEMPTATION.**
   Jesus faced down temptation by telling the devil the truth, namely, only God is Lord. Consider using a contemporary version of Jesus' words: "God's in charge here, not you."

EVERYDAY STUFF

Even Jesus faced temptation when the devil confronted him in the wilderness.

5 TELL THE DEVIL TO GO BACK TO HELL.

Consider saying this: "You're right, Mr. Devil. I'm a sinner. Unfortunately, you have no power here. My Lord loves sinners and has forgiven me forever. There's nothing you can do about it. Go back to where you came from and quit bothering me!"

CAUTION!

The following step should be reserved for the rare occasions when the above methods fail and should only be attempted under the counsel of authority.

6 COMMIT SOME MINOR SIN TO THROW THE DEVIL OFF.

Unchecked temptation often leads to apathy, confusion, and even despair, which is the archenemy of faith. To thwart this process, commit a minor sin to remind yourself that Jesus came specifically to save *you* from sin. Don't forget to include this sin in your later confession. (Luther sometimes advised people to do this—especially those in danger of despair.)

BE AWARE

] There are different kinds of temptation. Regardless of the type, temptation always involves a hidden voice whispering to you, "Whatever God says, you really need to trust me instead. I'm the only thing that can help you."

] Temptations try to make us trust in ourselves or in other things more than in God. When you realize this, you'll see that everything on the list above is just turning back to Jesus who died to show you how much you can trust him.

HOW TO CARE FOR THE SICK

While a trained and licensed physician must be sought to treat illness and injury, there is no malady that cannot be helped with faithful attention and prayer.

1 ASSESS THE NATURE OF THE PROBLEM.
Visit a local pharmacy if the illness is a simple one. Over-the-counter medications usually provide temporary relief until the body heals itself. If symptoms persist, the sick person should see a doctor and get a more detailed diagnosis.

2 PRAY FOR THEM.
Intercessory prayers are prayers made on someone else's behalf. Recent studies point to healing in hospitalized patients who have been prayed for—even when the sick were not aware of the prayers. Add the afflicted person to your church's prayer list.

3 CALL IN THE ELDERS.
Prayer and emotional support from friends and family are vital parts of healing, living with illness, and facing death. Ask the pastor to assemble the church elders (leaders) for prayer and the laying on of hands.

Here's what the Bible says on this topic: "Are any among you sick? They should call for the elders of the church and have them pray over them, anointing them with oil in the name of the Lord" (James 5:14).

BE AWARE

] Many people claim expertise in healing, from acupuncturists and herbalists to "faith healers" and psychics. Use caution and skepticism, but keep an open mind.

] Many people believe that much healing can be found in "comfort foods," such as homemade chicken soup.

] Those who attempt to diagnose and treat their own symptoms can often do more harm than good. When in doubt, always consult a pharmacist, doctor, or other medical professional.

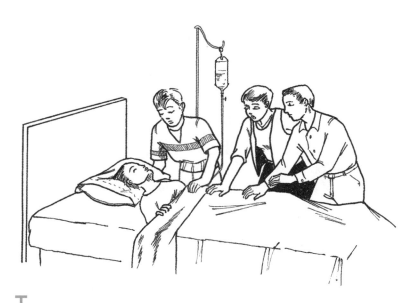

Gather friends, family, and church leaders to pray and lay hands on sick people.

HOW TO IDENTIFY AND AVOID EVIL

The devil delights in unnoticed evil. To this end, the devil employs a wide array of lies, disguises, and deceptions while attacking our relationships with God and each other. A sharp eye and vigilance are your best defense. Lutherans dislike the subject of evil, but many secretly cultivate extraordinary talent for rooting it out.

1 **KNOW YOUR ENEMY.**
Evil appears in many forms, most often using camouflage to present itself as kindly or friendly. Cruelty, hatred, violence, and exploitation are among the many forms evil can take, but it often masquerades as justice or something done "for their own good." Be alert to acts, people, and events that employ these methods, even if the eventual outcome appears good.

2 **PROCEED CAREFULLY AND DELIBERATELY.**
Avoid rushing to conclusions. Use good judgment.

3 **TAKE ACTION TO EXPOSE THE EVIL.**
Evil relies on darkness. It wants to remain hidden and hates the light of truth. Things that suffer from public knowledge or scrutiny might be evil.

4 **BE PREPARED TO MAKE A PERSONAL SACRIFICE.**
Fighting evil can be costly. A successful counterattack may require you to give up something you cherish. For Jesus, as for many of his followers, it was his life. Love is the foundation of sacrifice that combats evil.

5 STAY VIGILANT.

Evil's genius is shown in disguise, deception, and misdirection. Maintain your objectivity and apply the biblical measures of right and wrong you know to be correct. Martin Luther's standard was a conscience informed by Scripture and good common sense.

HOW TO AVOID GOSSIP

Gossip is among the most corrosive forces within a community and should be monitored closely. Discovery of gossip should be viewed as an opportunity to defend your neighbors' integrity, both gossiper and gossipee.

1 DETERMINE WHETHER THE CONVERSATION AT HAND QUALIFIES AS GOSSIP.

- Gossip involves one party speaking about a second party to a third party.

- The person who is the topic of gossip is not a participant in the conversation.

- The tone of the conversation is often secretive or negative. Gasps and whispers are common.

- The facts expressed in a gossip conversation are often unsubstantiated and have been obtained second- or third-hand.

2 RECALL AND HEED TITUS 3:2: "SPEAK EVIL OF NO ONE."

3 INTERJECT YOURSELF INTO THE CONVERSATION POLITELY.

Ask whether the gossiper(s) have spoken directly to the person about whom they are talking. If not, politely ask why. This may give some indication why they are gossiping.

4 MAKE A STATEMENT OF FACT.

Gossip withers in the face of truth. Make an attempt to parse out what is truly known from conjecture and supposition. State aloud that gossip is disrespectful and unfair.

Avoid gossip. It undermines community and damages relationships.

5 OFFER AN ALTERNATIVE EXPLANATION BASED ON FACT.

Describe other situations that cast the gossipee in a favorable light. Always try to give people the benefit of the doubt.

BE AWARE

] There is a fine line between helping and meddling. Pay close attention to your own motivations and the possible outcomes of your actions.

] Gossip injures both the gossiper and the person who is the subject of rumors.

] Consult the Eighth Commandment and its explanation in Martin Luther's Small Catechism on page 297.

] For further help, consult James 4:11.

EVERYDAY STUFF

HOW TO BLESS SOMEONE

Blessings through history have had many purposes, often involving the passing of wealth or property from one person or generation to another. A Christian blessing is a declaration of the gospel of Jesus Christ to a specific individual—an affirmation that another person is claimed and loved by almighty God. Blessings should be dispensed liberally and with abandon.

1 EVALUATE THE NEED AT HAND.
People have different needs at different times. When you perceive a need in which a blessing appears appropriate, take time to discern.

2 USE SAFE TOUCH.
Human touch is an affirmation with profound physical effects. Healing and emotional release are common. Make sure you use touch that is non-threatening, respectful, and communicates the love of Christ.

3 CHOOSE AN APPROPRIATE WAY TO GIVE THE BLESSING.
- Position one or both hands on the person's head. Use a light touch, but one firm enough to let the person know that he or she is being blessed.

- Place one hand on the person's shoulder.

- Trace a cross on the person's forehead.

- Hold both of the person's hands in yours while making good eye contact.

4   MAKE A DECLARATION OF FREEDOM.

- Blessings are often most effective when the spoken word is employed. For example: "[insert name here], child of God, you have been sealed by the Holy Spirit and marked with the cross of Christ forever."

- Consider ad-libbing a verbal blessing that speaks directly to the situation.

- Whenever possible, include the words spoken at baptism: "In the name of the Father, and of the Son, and of the Holy Spirit."

BE AWARE

] Indirect blessings are often appropriate. These include but are not limited to favors, prayers, kind words, consolation, a hot meal, shared laughter, and acceptance.

] Some cultures consider head-touching impolite or even rude, so always ask permission before making a blessing this way.

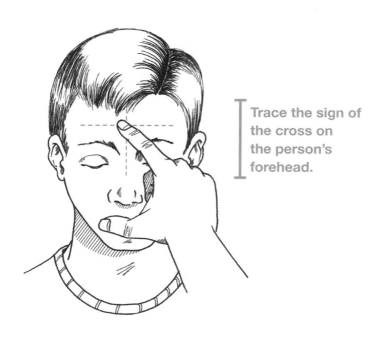

Trace the sign of the cross on the person's forehead.

HOW TO RESOLVE INTERPERSONAL CONFLICT

Disagreements are part of life. They often occur when we forget that not everyone sees things the same way. Conflict should be viewed as an opportunity to grow, not a contest for domination. Lutherans are traditionally shy, but when push comes to shove they value healthy relationships above all.

1 **ADOPT A HEALTHY ATTITUDE.**
Your frame of mind is critical. Approach the situation with forethought and calm. Prayer can be invaluable at this stage. Do not approach the other party when you're angry or upset.

2 **READ MATTHEW 18:15-20 BEFOREHAND.**
Consult the Bible to orient your thinking. This is the model Jesus provided and can be used to call to mind an appropriate method.

3 **TALK DIRECTLY TO THE PERSON INVOLVED.**
Avoid "triangulation." Talking about someone to a third party can make the conflict worse, as the person may feel that he or she is the subject of gossip. Speaking with the other person directly eliminates the danger and boosts the odds of a good outcome.

4 **EXPRESS YOURSELF WITHOUT ATTACKING.**
Using "I statements" can avoid casting the other person as the "bad guy" and inflaming the conflict. "I statements" are sentences beginning with phrases such as "I feel . . ." or "I'm uncomfortable when . . ."

5 KEEP "SPEAKING THE TRUTH IN LOVE" (EPHESIANS 4:15) AS YOUR GOAL.

Your "truth" may not be the other party's. Your objective is to discover and honor each other's "truth," not to put down the other person. Be ready to admit your own faults and mistakes.

6 SEEK OUT A THIRD PARTY TO ACT AS AN IMPARTIAL WITNESS.

If direct conversation doesn't resolve the conflict, locate someone both parties trust to sit in. This can help clarify your positions and bring understanding.

7 BUILD TOWARD FORGIVENESS AND A RENEWED FRIENDSHIP.

Agree upon how you will communicate to prevent future misunderstandings.

BE AWARE

] Seemingly unrelated events in your or the other person's life may be playing an invisible role in the conflict at hand. Be ready to shift the focus to the real cause.

] You may not be able to resolve the conflict at this time, but don't give up on future opportunities.

When two people aren't getting along, sometimes an impartial third person can help resolve the dispute.

HOW TO CONSOLE SOMEONE

Consolation is a gift from God. Christians in turn give it to others to build up the body of Christ and preserve it in times of trouble. (See 2 Corinthians 1:4-7.) Lutherans often employ food as a helpful secondary means.

1 **LISTEN FIRST.**
Make it known that you're present and available.

When the person opens up, be quiet and attentive.

2 **BE READY TO HELP THE PERSON FACE GRIEF AND SADNESS, NOT AVOID THEM.**
The object is to help the person name, understand, and work through his or her feelings, not gloss over them.

3 **AVOID SAYING THINGS TO MAKE YOURSELF FEEL BETTER.**
"I know exactly how you feel," is seldom true and trivializes the sufferer's pain. Even if you have experienced something similar, no experience is exactly the same. If there is nothing to say, simply be present with the person.

4 **SHOW RESPECT WITH HONESTY.**
Don't try to answer the mysteries of the universe or force your beliefs on the person. Be clear about the limitations of your abilities. Be ready to let some questions go unanswered. Consolation isn't about having all the answers, it's about bearing one another's burdens.

5 **DON'T PUT WORDS IN GOD'S MOUTH.**
Avoid saying, "This is God's will," or, "This is part of God's plan." Unless you heard it straight from God, don't say it.

HOW TO COPE WITH LOSS AND GRIEF

Lutherans tend to downplay their losses by saying, "Well, it could be worse." This may provide only temporary relief at best. Any loss can cause pain, feelings of confusion, and uncertainty. These responses are normal.

1 **FAMILIARIZE YOURSELF WITH THE STAGES OF GRIEF.**
Experts identify five: denial, anger, bargaining, depression, and acceptance. Some add hope as a sixth stage. Grieving persons cycle back and forth through the stages, sometimes experiencing two or three in a single day. This is normal.

2 **EXPRESS YOUR GRIEF.**
Healthy ways may include crying, staring into space for extended periods, ruminating, shouting at the ceiling, and sudden napping. Laughing outbursts are also appropriate and should not be judged harshly.

3 **IDENTIFY SOMEONE YOU TRUST TO TALK TO.**
Available people can include a spouse, parents, relatives, friends, a pastor, a doctor, or a trained counselor. Many household pets also make good listeners and willing confidants.

4 **CHOOSE A PERSONAL WAY TO MEMORIALIZE THE LOSS.**
Make a collage of photographs, offer a memorial donation to your church, or start a scrapbook of memories to honor the event. This helps you to begin to heal without getting stuck in your grief.

EVERYDAY STUFF

BE AWARE

] Many experts prescribe a self-giving activity, such as volunteering at a shelter or soup kitchen, as a means of facilitating a healthy grieving process.

] The pain immediately after suffering a loss is usually deep and intense. This will lessen with the passage of time.

] Anger, guilt, bitterness, and sadness are likely emotions.

] Short-term depression may occur in extreme cases. After experiencing a great loss, such as the death of a loved one, make an appointment with your family physician for a physical.

] Even Jesus cried when his friend Lazarus died (John 11:35).

Even Jesus felt the loss of Lazarus when he died.

Mary   Martha

THE TOP 10 ATTRIBUTES TO LOOK FOR IN A SPOUSE

While no single personality trait can predict a compatible marriage, the following list frames the basic things to look for in a spouse. With all attributes, some differences can be the source of a couple's strength rather than a source of difficulty. Statistically, Lutherans appear to be about as successful at choosing a spouse as other people.

1 SIMILAR VALUES

Values that concern religious beliefs, life purpose, financial priorities, and children are a foundation on which to build the relationship. Contrary values tend to create discord.

2 PHYSICAL-ENERGY AND PHYSICAL-SPACE COMPATIBILITY

Consider whether the person's energy level and physical-space needs work with yours. Also, the word *compatibility* can mean a complementary match of opposites, or it can denote a match based on strong similarities.

3 PHYSICAL AND ROMANTIC COMPATIBILITY

If the two of you have a similar degree of interest in or need for physical and romantic expression in your relationship, the chance of lifelong compatibility increases.

4 INTELLECTUAL PARITY

Communicating with someone who has a significantly different intelligence level or educational background can require extra effort.

5 EMOTIONAL MATURITY

A lifelong relationship of mutual challenge and support often helps each person grow emotionally, but a lifetime spent waiting for someone to grow up could be more frustration than it's worth.

6 SENSE OF HUMOR

Sense of humor can provide an excellent measure of a person's personality and an important means to couple survival. If he or she doesn't get your jokes, you could be asking for trouble.

7 RESPECT

Look for someone who listens to you without trying to control you. Look also for a healthy sense of self-respect.

8 TRUSTWORTHINESS

Seek out someone who is honest and acts with your best interests in mind—not only his or hers—and tries to learn from his or her mistakes.

9 FORGIVING

When you sincerely apologize to your spouse, he or she should try to work through and get beyond the problem rather than hold on to it. Once forgiven, past mistakes should not be raised, especially in conflict situations.

10 KINDNESS

An attitude of consistent kindness may be the most critical attribute for a lifelong partnership.

BE AWARE

] If you live to be old, you will probably experience major changes that you cannot predict at age 15 or 25 or 35. Accepting this fact in advance can help you weather difficult times.

] Use all of your resources—intuition, emotions, and rational thought—to make the decision about a life partner.

] Family members and trusted friends can offer invaluable advice in this decision-making process and should be consulted.

EVERYDAY STUFF

HOW TO BE SAVED (BY GRACE THROUGH FAITH AND NOT BY YOUR GOOD WORKS)

Many religions are built on the idea that the more closely people follow the religious rules or the more morally people behave, the better God will like them—and the better God likes them, the greater their chances of "getting into heaven."

While there is nothing wrong with moral living or obeying God's laws, that kind of behavior has very little to do with the salvation God offers. You don't need to be a follower of Jesus Christ for that.

Christianity, on the other hand, says that out of pure love God was willing to sacrifice everything—even his only Son—to save you forever from sin, death, and all your false gods. Including you.

Since God has already done everything needed to secure your salvation through Jesus, you never have to do one single thing to earn God's favor, no matter how bad you are at following the rules. Still, being saved takes some getting used to.

1 **GET FAMILIAR WITH THE WORD "GRACE."**
   Grace means that God gives you all the good stuff—forgiveness, salvation, love, and life, with all its ups and downs—as totally free gifts. Keep an eye out for situations in which you can use this word, and then use it liberally. You'll soon begin to see God's grace all around you.

2 PRACTICE LETTING GO OF THINGS YOU LOVE.

Staying focused on yourself can make it difficult to open up to a grace-filled world. But giving of yourself, your time, and your possessions can put you in a receptive, open frame of mind. This is important, as salvation cannot be "found" by looking for it, it is only revealed.

3 LOSE YOURSELF AS OFTEN AS POSSIBLE.

An important part of having a receptive frame of mind is losing yourself in whatever you're doing. To do this, give yourself over entirely to the activity. This can be accomplished in prayer and worship, but also through things like playing games, talking with friends and family, reading a good book, serving others, or playing a musical instrument. Even work can accomplish this.

4 ADMIT YOUR LIMITATIONS.

Without straying into despair or false modesty, make an honest confession to yourself about what you can and cannot do, what you are and what you are not. When you see yourself realistically you become more open to God's message of love, grace, and salvation.

5 ACCEPT YOUR UNIQUENESS.

In God's eyes, you were so valuable as to merit the ultimate sacrifice of his Son, even before you spoke your first words. God will spend your whole life trying to convince you of this. When you accept that to God you are priceless beyond imagining it becomes easier to understand why God chose to save you.

6 SPEND TIME IN WORSHIP AND PRAYER TO THE LIVING GOD.

While only God grants the faith that saves, the church gives lots of opportunities where God has promised to come to you.

EVERYDAY STUFF

7 AVOID THE TEMPTATION TO "DO."

The "old Adam" or "old Eve" in you—the sinner in you—
always wants to be in charge over God. He or she will tell you
that God's grace is too good to be true and that you must
"do" something to earn or justify it. Simply remind him or
her that you were baptized into Jesus Christ and have all the
grace you need.

BE AWARE

] The apostle Paul's summary of the gospel goes like this: "For
by grace you have been saved through faith, and this is not
your own doing; it is the gift of God—not the result of works,
so that no one may boast" (Ephesians 2:8-9).

] This viewpoint about God's grace, even among many Christians, is unpopular, as it was when Martin Luther and the
reformers reminded the church of it almost 500 years ago. Be
aware that once you adopt it you will come under fire and be
tempted to lapse back into the old way.

GRACE

Getting familiar with
this very important
word will help you get
used to being saved.

HOW TO REFORM THE CHURCH WHEN IT STRAYS FROM THE GOSPEL

When Martin Luther nailed his Ninety-five Theses to the church door in 1517, he took a stand against the corruption he saw in the church—false gospels, immoral leaders, and bad theology—and launched the Reformation.

From then on, by hanging on to his belief that only the free gift of faith in Christ could save him—and that the institutional church could not—Luther took a stand for an idea that survives today: *Ecclesia semper reformanda est.* (This means, "The church must always reform.")

To stay faithful to the gospel, the church still depends on all its members to call it back, not to their own personal visions, but to Jesus' vision.

1 **KNOW YOUR STUFF.**
   You can't call the church back to the gospel if you don't learn for yourself what the gospel is. Read your Bible regularly. Also, spend time in conversation with good theologians, like pastors and church elders.

2 **TRUST YOUR CONSCIENCE, BUT EQUIP IT FIRST WITH GOOD INFORMATION.**
   To defy corrupt church authorities, Luther had to draw strength from even more powerful sources, namely his faith in God and his conscience. "It is neither safe nor right," he said, "to go against conscience."

3 **DOUBLE-CHECK AND TRIPLE-CHECK YOUR MOTIVATIONS. ARE YOU FIGHTING ON BEHALF OF THE GOSPEL OR FOR YOUR OWN PERSONAL AGENDA?**
Knowing the difference between the two matters. Some things may be worthy social causes that deserve your time and attention, but they may not be the gospel.

4 **SPEAK OUT. ACT.**
It isn't enough just to take a stand or hold an opinion. Once you're sure you're doing it for the right reasons, find an effective way to make change happen.

Luther nailed the Ninety-five Theses in a public place (a common way to speak to the public in his day) and later used the printing press to spread his opinions to the widest possible audience. He put himself in the line of fire.

5 **PREPARE TO DEFEND YOURSELF, AND YOUR MESSAGE OF REFORM, FROM ATTACK.**
People tend to dislike reform—and institutions like it even less. While the church calls us to model the love of Christ and live by his teachings, sometimes the church and its leaders respond to reformers with a "kill the messenger" attitude.

6 **KEEP STEADY, BE PATIENT, AND LISTEN TO WISE COUNSEL.**
The Reformation took decades to take root. During that time, Luther and other reformers battled church authorities. They also debated with each other about the best way to bring the gospel to a new age and restore the church to its real purpose.

BE AWARE

] Not all efforts at reforming the church succeed. Refer to "How to Avoid Getting Burned at the Stake" on page 64 for more information.

HOW TO ENCOUNTER
THE HOLY TRINITY AS ONE
GOD IN THREE PERSONS

The Trinity is a mystery. Even great theologians don't completely understand, and some scholars spend their whole lives studying it. After 2,000 years, Christians still believe in this mystery because it gives life and shape to everything in our lives—our relationships, our faith, and especially our worship.

1   **GET TO KNOW THE THREE TRINITARIAN CREEDS: THE NICENE CREED, THE ATHANASIAN CREED, AND THE APOSTLES' CREED. CONSIDER MEMORIZING EACH ONE (TWO OF THEM ARE PRETTY LONG).**
    These three "symbols," as they are sometimes called, were written during different times of crisis when heresies threatened the church's unity and clear statements about what Christians believed were needed. While different from each other, they each teach a lot about the three-personed God.

A triangle is often used to represent the Holy Trinity—one God in three persons.

A triangle is often used to represent the Holy Trinity—one God in three persons.

Father

Holy Spirit

Son

2 INCLUDE THE SIGN OF THE CROSS AND THE BAPTISMAL WORDS AS A REGULAR PART OF YOUR PRAYER LIFE AND WORSHIP LIFE.

The sign of the cross goes with the words, "In the name of the Father, and of the Son, and of the Holy Spirit," which traces a physical reminder of the Trinity on your body. For more information on making the sign of the cross, refer to the diagram on page 206.

3 UNDERSTAND THAT YOU WERE MADE IN GOD'S IMAGE.

Just as the one God is Father, Son, and Holy Spirit all at once, you are mind, body, and soul all at once. Because you reflect the image of God you were made to live a life of worship in which everything you do and say honors God.

4 SPEND TIME IN THE COMMUNITY OF FAITH.

Go to worship, fellowship, Bible study, Sunday school, and anything else that regularly keeps you in the company of other Christians.

5 SEEK OUT GOD'S WORD AND THE MEANS OF GRACE.

The Trinity is revealed in reading the Bible, preaching, the Sacraments, the forgiveness of sins, the community of believers, and within anything else where Jesus, the living Word, is active.

BE AWARE

] Some people use handy metaphors to begin to get a handle on the doctrine of the Trinity. For example, water takes three major forms: liquid, solid, and gas. Yet it remains one substance. Such metaphors are very useful to a point, but ultimately they must give way to the divine mystery that remains.

HOW TO TELL THE DIFFERENCE BETWEEN THEOLOGY OF THE CROSS AND THEOLOGY OF GLORY

Distinguishing between cross and glory theologies requires a keen mind and the ability to differentiate between law and gospel. Like other Lutheran concepts, this one is difficult to quantify because it is actually a *way of thinking* rather than a strict set of rules. Luckily, the learning curve is quite short due to the abundance of theology of glory in our world and culture.

1 **PAY EXTREMELY CLOSE ATTENTION TO THE USE OF LANGUAGE.**
Lutherans are famous for overparsing other people's sentence structure, but this arises from a valuable theological instinct. Who is the actor in this case? What did they do? How was their action described? Who benefits? Who receives the glory for it? While these questions all sound like political suspicion they're actually a right-headed effort to expose theology of glory and keep the focus on Christ.

2 **REMAIN VIGILANT AGAINST THE IMPLICATION THAT HUMAN BEINGS ARE ALL-POWERFUL, ESPECIALLY WITH RESPECT TO THEIR OWN SALVATION FROM SIN AND DEATH.**
Theologians of glory vastly overestimate a person's innate ability to believe and do the things necessary to gain access to God's grace—access that only God, through Jesus Christ, can grant. While perhaps not always consciously, they conceive of their own will as primary and God's as peripheral. They love sentences that begin with the pronoun "I."*

3 **TRAIN YOUR MIND TO FAVOR GOD OVER HUMAN BEINGS AS THE "SUBJECT OF THE SENTENCE."**

The theology of the cross claims the cross of Christ as a complete break from human "religious" efforts. That is, the cross represents *God's* decision and work for humans apart from any human action. Theologies of glory, on the other hand, nearly always emphasize human decision or work. Put simply, a theology of glory puts you in the driver's seat while a theology of the cross confesses that God does it all through the cross.

4   **USE THE CHART ON THE NEXT PAGE AS A MEANS OF ORIENTING YOUR MIND TOWARD DISTINGUISHING THE TWO THEOLOGIES.**

BE AWARE

]   Once you start looking for theologies of glory you begin to see them everywhere. One excellent example is in the movie *Indiana Jones and The Last Crusade* (1989). In the climactic scene, Indy must solve a series of booby-trapped puzzles to reach the Holy Grail. Before he can obtain the "Cup of the Carpenter" he has to "prove his worth" by (1) bowing in penance, (2) following in the footsteps of God's proper name, (3) taking a leap of faith, and (4) selecting the true grail from dozens of false ones. This represents a typical theology of glory: God's salvation—in this case, the healing cup—can only be attained by proper human decision and effort.

]   When you relapse into theology of glory, as everyone does occasionally, avoid punishing yourself. Simply recognize it, go back, and start again.

]   Luckily, it is not our theologies that save us, but Jesus Christ.

*Many theologians of glory become experts at camouflaging this move by confusing the words "I" and "God." In other words, beginning sentences with the word "God" does not *necessarily* make the statement one of theology of the cross. For example, "God told me to hit my sister," could be used to cloak unsavory ulterior motives. It is highly unlikely that God actually told you to hit your sister.

Theology of Glory item	Why it's a Theology of Glory
Songs with lines like "Still the greatest treasure remains for those who gladly choose you now."	These songs glorify the one singing—and "choosing"—rather than the one to whom the song is being sung.
The claim from "religious" persons that you must somehow become less sinful and more saintly before God will accept you.	This suggests that it's up to you to become worthy to receive God's grace; this opposes the fact that while we were God's enemies, "we were reconciled to God through the death of his Son" (Romans 5:10).
The "religious" insistence that you must "decide" to accept Jesus as your Lord and Savior before he can save you.	If it's up to you to decide to be saved then you are not being saved by Jesus. Instead, you are saving yourself by virtue of your perceived ability to make the right decision.
Explanations for untimely deaths and other tragedies, like, "God took her because he needed another angel in heaven," or, "The Lord allowed his death in order to prevent greater suffering."	Theologians of glory typically believe they can get inside God's mind, forgetting the part where God says, "My thoughts are not your thoughts, nor are your ways my ways" (Isaiah 55:8).
The claim that the Bible contains a code about future events and that you can know exactly how these future events will play out.	The only thing certain about Christian "millennialism," as this view is known, is that for two millennia Christians have attempted to predict the future and for two millennia these predictions have been wrong.
Claims regarding who is going to heaven and who is going to that other place.	In the Apostles' Creed, Christians confess that Jesus will "come again to judge the living and the dead." Only a theologian of glory is presumptuous enough to take over a role that properly belongs to Christ.

Much better to sing about what Christ has done, is doing, and will do *for you*, rather than to boast about what you have done, are doing, or will do for Christ.

As Luther observed, "The Love of God does not find, but creates that which is pleasing to it."

"Free will after the fall exists in name only," Luther said. Human will is bound to choose against God and only God can free the mind and heart for faith.

"That person does not deserve to be called a theologian who looks upon the invisible things of God as though they were clearly perceptible in those things which have actually happened," Luther famously said.

God acts most often "behind-the-scenes," doing work that we cannot know. The apostle Paul's confession: "O the depth of the riches and wisdom and knowledge of God! How unsearchable are God's judgments and how inscrutable God's ways!" (Romans 11:33).

[Have fun and learn! Add your own!]

EVERYDAY STUFF

HOW TO BECOME A THEOLOGIAN OF THE CROSS (AND AVOID BEING A THEOLOGIAN OF GLORY)

The term *theologian* technically means a student of or specialist in theology. And *theology* is the study of God and God's relationship with humanity and the universe. You may not consider yourself a specialist yet, but you definitely are a student of theology. To do this well, you may wish to follow in the footsteps of Martin Luther, who brought the Christian church away from a misguided "theology of glory" and back to the "theology of the cross."

1 POSITION THE CROSS IN YOUR THINKING AS AN END POINT, NOT A STARTING POINT.

The cross of Jesus Christ is the most important and powerful thing in Christian faith. But it's easy to misunderstand what this means. A "theologian of glory," based on nothing more than individual wishes, tries to use the cross as a starting point for personal gain—to make people healthy and wealthy, successful and popular. A "theologian of the cross," in contrast, thinks of the cross as the last stop for sin, death, and delusions of grandeur. In other words, the cross is an end point.

2 DETERMINE TO BECOME A THEOLOGIAN OF THE CROSS.

The apostle Paul explains this approach: "For I decided to know nothing among you except Jesus Christ and him crucified" (1 Corinthians 2).

3 IDENTIFY THE MARKS OF THE THEOLOGY OF GLORY AND PRACTICE CONTRASTING THEM WITH THE THEOLOGY OF THE CROSS.

A theologian of glory might say something like: "Accept Jesus as your personal Lord and Savior and he will make you happier, richer, and better looking." If things don't pan out, the theologian of glory will say that you need to have greater faith, believe more, or try harder.

A theologian of the cross, on the other hand, emphasizes what Jesus did for us. In baptism, Jesus gives you his word, which essentially says, "You are mine," even when you feel troubled, poor, or unattractive.

4 LOOK FOR GOD TO REVEAL HIMSELF IN THE MOST UNEXPECTED PLACES.

A theologian of glory thinks that God shows up where humans expect God to show up: in things that are powerful, wise, and important by human standards. On the other hand, the theologian of the cross knows that God is much subtler: God shows up in those things that seem weak, foolish, and insignificant to human eyes. (See 1 Corinthians 1:17-29.)

5 ACCEPT THE LIFELONG NATURE OF BECOMING A THEOLOGIAN OF THE CROSS.

In the end, being a theologian of the cross is something that can't be taught from a book. There's no class you can take or diploma you can get that certifies you as a theologian of the cross. As you experience life's ups and downs, being a theologian of the cross is something you just live into when you are open and trust God's promises.

EVERYDAY STUFF

HOW TO RECEIVE GOD'S GRACE DAILY

God's grace exists in a dual, paradoxical state that many Protestant theologians describe as being *transcendent and immanent*—that is, above and beyond the realm of human understanding, but also ever-present and constantly available to human beings. One suggested analogy involves the human as a radio, "tuned in" to God's grace the same way a dial is set to a constant, pre-existing signal.

1 **DON'T DO ANYTHING.**
Receiving God's grace doesn't depend on what you do or how much you believe. Grace can be received only as a free gift from God through Jesus Christ.

2 **AVOID FRANTIC SEEKING, SEARCHING, OR STRIVING.**
The word *receive* implies a key stance of passivity befitting the recipient of a gift. Grace is a revealed gift; it cannot be commanded, controlled, or earned.

3 **STAY POSITIVE.**
Certain attitudes of the recipient make grace easier to recognize. These include: thankfulness, obedience, and not being invested in the outcome of situations. It can, in part, be described by this phrase from the Lord's Prayer: "Your will be done."

4 **REMAIN SPIRITUALLY STILL; PRACTICE STILLNESS IN ALL ITS FORMS.**
Grace, coming from God, is often received and perceived in quiet moments that allow the "still small voice" of God to speak a peace that passes understanding.

God's grace has been compared to a kind of omnipresent, ever-present radio signal to which human beings can be tuned.

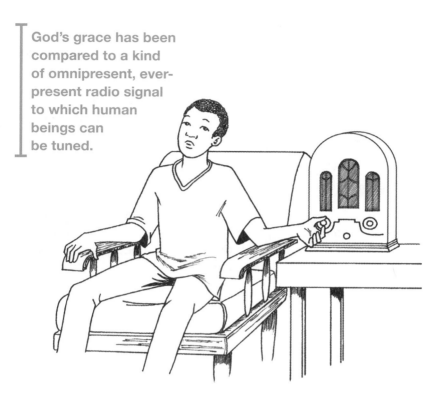

5   UTILIZE PRAYER AS A MEANS TO TUNE YOUR DIAL TO THE RIGHT SIGNAL.

Meditative prayer is often best, as it encourages the values mentioned above, but the beloved Serenity Prayer is a viable linguistic means: "God grant me the serenity to accept the things I cannot change; courage to change the things I can; and wisdom to know the difference."

EVERYDAY STUFF

BE AWARE

] For Lutherans, God's grace is both *hidden* and *revealed* at the same time.

] God's grace is clearly *visible*, however, in the life, death, and resurrection of Jesus Christ. For confirmation of God's love for you, direct your attention to the cross.

] Receiving God's grace is not contingent on the results of a pass-fail behavior test.

] The Rev. James Jones, Bishop of Liverpool, explains grace thusly: "The best thing about grace is that God loves you just as you are. That is truly wonderful, that is good news for any human being on the face of this planet."

HOW TO PROCLAIM THE GOSPEL TO SOMEONE WHO NEEDS TO HEAR IT

Christian belief puts overwhelming stress on the Word and preaching the gospel to others through a verbal declaration. For Lutherans, this declaration is the thing sinners afflicted by the law hunger and wait and listen for; learning how to declare it in life situations, therefore, is a critical skill that requires both practice and boldness.

1 **ASSESS THE HUMAN NEED AT HAND.**
   Is the person hungry? Lonely? Depressed? Diseased? Spiritual needs can become manifest through physical, behavioral or psychological symptoms. Most often the affliction is the result of some law or other having remorselessly gone to work on the person.

2 **AVOID NEGLECTING THE PHYSICAL OPPORTUNITIES TO BRING THE GOSPEL.**
   Although he delivered many sermons and teachings and was himself God's forgiveness and salvation for sinners, Christ's ministry was physically dynamic: he washed feet, cleansed lepers, healed the sick, and raised the dead. When such physical acts accompany an authentic delivery of the gospel, the impact is more than double.

3 **REMAIN HUMBLE. AVOID FOISTING.**
   Preaching the gospel in one-on-one situations is a holy moment in which God is at work. Assume a self-effacing but firm stance, which is likely to result in an open, inviting listener. Use direct, true, conversational language. Syrupy, over-the-top, disingenuous Jesus-talk is likely to ring hollow to skeptical listeners, especially hard-bitten Lutherans.

The gospel is usually best proclaimed in words aimed directly at another person's situation in which freedom in Jesus Christ and liberation from sin are particularly needed.

4 DECLARE THE GOSPEL ALOUD AND WITHOUT RESERVATION.

Say, "The devil assaults you with this law because he knows Christ lives in you through your baptism. Jesus died on the cross to put that devil under his foot and raise you up into a new life. You are forgiven." Or something along those lines.

5 FOLLOW THROUGH.

Just as Christ built a relationship with you, try maintaining a relationship with those to whom you declare the gospel whenever possible. Multiple declarations will probably be required, especially to those unfamiliar with the language of faith.

BE AWARE

] Sinners also need to hear the law, but clearly defined. Proclamation of the gospel is most effective when preceded by
clarification that names the Old Adam or Old Eve in them.

] Blanket proclamations of judgment, hellfire, condemnation,
along with scriptural citations, shaming, or using the voice
and cadence of a televangelist (particularly by drawing out the
name *Jeeee-sus*) will almost always achieve a negative result.

The gospel can be preached in deed as well in the form of physical acts of kindness that speak where words alone might not suffice.

THE TOP THREE USES OF THE LAW

"You shall have no other gods." That's the First Commandment. There are more than 600 additional commands in the first five books of the Old Testament. Additionally, there are dozens of rules in the New Testament, such as Jesus' request, "Just as I have loved you, you also should love one another" (John 13:34), and "pray without ceasing" (1 Thessalonians 5:17). Lutherans have always understood that the law has particular functions, also called "uses."

1 THE FIRST USE OF THE LAW

Latin term: *usus civilis* ("civil use").

At face value, laws simply let us know what is required of us in terms of conduct. The law, therefore, is first given in order to maintain discipline so our sinful impulses are kept in check, order is maintained, and human community can be possible.

The first use of the law is to restrain sin and evil and keep good order.

2 THE SECOND USE OF THE LAW

Latin term: *Usus pedegogicus* ("pedagogical use").

The law *teaches* us (a) that we always fall short of keeping it, (b) that we are sinners, and (c) that we need someone to save us from sin and its consequences. That is, the law's second use drives us to Christ and his cross. For Lutherans this use is the most important use because it leads to salvation.

3 THE THIRD USE OF THE LAW

Latin term: *usus tertius* ("third use").

Most Lutherans believe that after one becomes a Christian, the law is still necessary. "Third Users" believe that apart from the first use a third use must be applied in order to establish a Christian pattern of life. "Non-Third Users" argue that the third use is redundant and unnecessary, saying the first use gives Christians all they need in this regard.

Like a tough teacher, the second use of the law truthfully instructs us as to our sinful nature and drives us always toward Jesus Christ who is our salvation.

LIFE REPORT CARD

NOT SINNING — F
TRUSTING GOD — D-
OBEYING PARENTS — D
FOLLOWING COMMANDMENTS — F-
DEFENDING NEIGHBORS — D
DOING GOOD WORKS — D-
FAITH IN JESUS — F-
CONDEMNING SATAN — F

Please see Jesus immediately!

BE AWARE

] Lutherans generally agree about the first two uses of the law. The third use has been a bone of contention, however. In 1580, a group of second-generation Lutherans attempted to reach a concord on the issue, but the issue persists even today.

] There are only three known uses of the law. There is no fourth or fifth use. Also no sixth use. Some archeologists thought they had uncovered a seventh use once, but they hadn't. No seventh use, either.

Some Lutherans argue for a third use of the law, which outlines and motivates a Christian pattern of life.

HOW TO TELL THE DIFFERENCE BETWEEN CHEAP GRACE AND REGULAR GRACE

The Lutheran understanding of grace is often summed up by Ephesians 2:8-9, "For by grace you have been saved through faith, and this is not your own doing; it is the gift of God—not the result of works, so that no one may boast." The term "cheap grace" applies when a person knowingly uses God's grace as a justification for sin—by commission or omission. The following rationales usually signal the presence of cheap grace:

1 **"I KNOW GOD WILL FORGIVE ME, SO I'M GOING TO _____ ANYWAY."**
   No sin is unforgivable. However, as Paul writes in Romans 2:4, "Do you realize that God's kindness is meant to lead us to repentance?"

2 **"JESUS THREW OUT THE OLD LAW AND MADE A NEW LAW."**
   Jesus conquered sin, death, and the power of the devil when he died and rose again. However, the law still applies. Jesus addressed this in his Sermon on the Mount when he said, "Do not think that I have come to abolish the law or the prophets; I have come not to abolish but to fulfill" (Matthew 5:17).

3 **"IT'S EASIER TO ASK FOR FORGIVENESS THAN PERMISSION."**
   If so, you're probably looking for a helping of cheap grace. Isaiah 66:2 says God looks to the "humble and contrite in spirit." God doesn't call us to go through the motions of asking forgiveness as a formality. People aren't truly "contrite" if they knew in advance they were about to do something wrong.

Regular grace is actually quite costly, as it has been paid for through Jesus' precious blood and innocent suffering and death in atonement for our sins. Regular grace is a free gift to you.

4 "SIN BOLDLY."

Many well-meaning Lutherans invoke this partial quote by Martin Luther to justify their sins. In fact, Luther intended to refute cheap grace when he said, "Sin boldly, but believe and rejoice in Christ even more boldly, for he is victorious over sin, death, and the world." Your identity in Christ is the critical thing; glossing over sin with half-truths only obscures this.

BE AWARE

] Humans manufacture cheap grace. Regular grace pops out of nowhere, undeserved, uncontrived, and dismantles all your self-justifications before Christ because it comes straight from God.

] Paul reminds us in Romans 6:1-2, "What then are we to say? Should we continue in sin in order that grace may abound? By no means! How can we who died to sin go on living in it?"

] *Antinomian* is a fancy word for someone who indulges in "cheap grace." (Anti = "against," Nomian = "law.")

Cheap grace is most often attended by a certain flip attitude and used as excuse or permission for sin. Cheap grace is manufactured by humans and costs nothing.

EVERYDAY STUFF

HOW TO REPENT

Christians regard repentance as a fundamental benefit of the Christian life. Jesus said, "The kingdom of God is near. Repent and believe the good news" (Mark 1:15). The New Testament word for repent means "to change one's mind," as in to change one's heart and life completely. The Old Testament word for repent means "to turn," as in to turn away from sin and back to God.

Repentance is about turning away from sin and turning back toward God. God calls us to repent both "once" in our lives and also "every day." Those who don't know the Lord repent "once"— to turn toward the Lord and be saved by God's grace. Those who already know the Lord repent "every day"—to turn away from the evil and sin that tempts us, and turn back to God. In both cases, the method of repentance is the same.

1 **HEAR GOD'S WORD.**
   God's Word instructs us about the sin in our lives. The Word shows us those things about us that are not of God. God's Word comes to us through Jesus, through the Scriptures, and through preaching.

2 **RECOGNIZE AND ADMIT YOUR SIN.**
   Part of repentance is acknowledging our sin and being sorry for the wrong we do: "Godly sorrow brings repentance" (2 Corinthians 7:10). Tell God you know you sin and that you are sorry for your sin.

3 **ASK THE HOLY SPIRIT FOR HELP TURNING BACK TO GOD.**
   A person cannot repent or turn to God on his or her own. Ask God for help. Pray in the name of Jesus that the Holy Spirit would come to you and turn you back to the Lord.

4 LIVE AS A FORGIVEN SINNER.
God wants us to live in the way that is best for us and best for our neighbors—a way that points to God. Live according to God's will, loving God and your neighbor with all your heart.

5 REPEAT THE PROCESS DAILY.
Repentance is a way of life. Every day brings new opportunities to hear God's Word, acknowledge and be sorry for the wrong we do, ask God for help, and live as forgiven sinners.

BE AWARE
] In cases when no particular sin can be called to mind, repentance should nonetheless be undertaken earnestly. Simply tell God that you are sorry for sins you are not aware of. You have certainly committed some.

HOW TO IDENTIFY A "NEIGHBOR" AND WHAT THIS MEANS FOR LUTHERANS

Luther's "neighbor" theology was firmly rooted in his belief in Jesus Christ, who came not to be served but to serve. Luther professed that as followers of Christ, each of us is called to be a "little Christ" to others. These "others" are our neighbors, whom God places in our lives on purpose. Important earmarks for recognizing a neighbor may include the following:

1 **LOOK FOR OBVIOUS SIGNS OF BEING IN NEED.**
   If you see someone in need, assume that person is a neighbor. Signs of need include hunger, lack of shelter, distress or anxiety, or destructive behavior patterns. People with poor fashion sense are neighbors but may require a lighter touch.

2 **APPLY A RECKLESS LACK OF DISCRIMINATION IN YOUR ANALYSIS.**
   Jesus ate with tax collectors and prostitutes. There is no universal profile for identifying a neighbor. Neighbors come in all shapes, sizes, colors, and ages and are often people you would least like to have as your neighbors. *Note:* Suffering unneighborly behavior from someone does not exempt you from regarding that person as a neighbor.

3 **PRACTICE RECEIVING OTHERS' NEIGHBORLINESS WITH GRACE.**
   Your own skills in identifying and serving your neighbor may improve as you focus on the extraordinary kindnesses you receive daily from those around you. Adopt an attitude of abundance in this regard.

4 MAKE A THOROUGH INVENTORY OF ALL NEIGHBORS WITHIN YOUR PERSONAL REACH.
Family members, roommates, coworkers, bad drivers, children, and convenience store clerks should be included in your list. Practice Christ-like neighborliness toward these people.

5 CONSIDER EXPANDING YOUR NEIGHBORLY SPHERE OF INFLUENCE.
The Internet has opened and expanded opportunities to recognize neighbors around the world and to serve them. Be vigilant in serving distant neighbors. Support global missions or world hunger programs to meet their needs.

6 DEFINE "NEIGHBOR" AS LIBERALLY AS POSSIBLE.
Strive to abandon stereotypes and to embrace the unfamiliar and weird. We cannot limit who we call "neighbor." God's love excludes no one.

BE AWARE

] Being a good neighbor can include actions other than sheer kindness.

] Focusing efforts regularly on defining yourself can help you become a better neighbor to others.

EVERYDAY STUFF

HOW TO ADOPT
AN EVANGELISTIC LIFESTYLE
WITHOUT ALIENATING PEOPLE

Some Christians believe adopting an evangelistic lifestyle means they must seek to drag people to church, a tactic that can backfire when applied injudiciously. Adopting an evangelistic lifestyle simply means living a life that reflects that the teachings of Jesus are active in your mind and heart.

1 **ADOPT AN ATTITUDE OF WELCOMING, PERSONAL HOSPITALITY, AND ACCEPTANCE.**
Jesus invited people of little status to join him wherever he was. He dined with sinners, tax collectors, and women—people who often were disregarded during biblical times. Follow Jesus' example.

2 **ACTIVELY SEEK OUT OPPORTUNITIES TO SERVE AS JESUS DID.**
When you live an evangelistic lifestyle, you actively look for ways to serve the needs of others and to treat all people as neighbors.

3 **INITIATE NATURAL AND UNFORCED FAITH CONVERSATIONS AS A MATTER OF HABIT.**
Talk about your faith journey and where it has led you. Compare notes with others without casting judgment. Avoid falling in love with the sound of your own voice or the repeated retelling of your life story. Attempt to learn something from everyone.

Unpretentiousness is a valuable ally when attempting to adopt an evangelistic lifestyle. Act casually.

4 CONSIDER WEARING SYMBOLS OF YOUR FAITH; AVOID CONTRIVED GARISHNESS.

Wear a tasteful cross necklace on a regular basis, but consider concealing it from time to time under clothing. Read the Bible during your lunch hour, but consider purchasing an edition with an unobtrusive cover. Displaying faith symbols offers others the opportunity to ask about them, but glaring announcements of Jesus' love can have an undesirable effect.

EVERYDAY STUFF

5 **ESTABLISH A HABIT OF WANTON FORGIVENESS.**
Everybody makes mistakes. Make forgiveness a foundation of your life. Forgiveness consumes less energy than anger or revenge, and it serves as a strong witness to God's work.

6 **MAINTAIN A RIGOROUS PRAYER SCHEDULE.**
An important foundation for an evangelistic lifestyle is regular conversations with God, which centers you for daily living.

BE AWARE

] Many people may have experienced "evangelistic" people as unnecessarily negative and judgmental. Use grace and forgiveness to counteract this negativism.

] How you act may be more important than what you say.

HOW TO TITHE

The Old Testament contains many references to tithing as the giving standard for God's people. A "tithe" (10th) is simply 10 percent of one's income given directly to fund God's work. Tithing requires a conscious decision, discipline, and sacrifice and may take a lifetime to achieve, but seasoned tithers report extraordinary spiritual dividends.

1 COMMIT TO THE GOAL OF GIVING 10 PERCENT, COME WHAT MAY.

Tithing requires fortitude and perseverance. Resolve not to waver; consider sealing your commitment with a ceremonial "first check" or a tattoo.

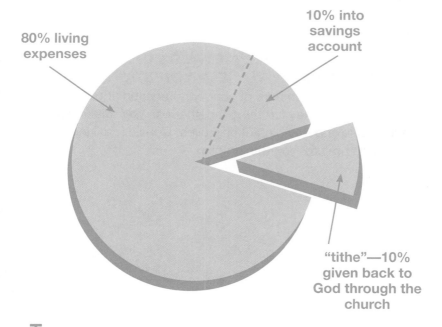

80% living expenses

10% into savings account

"tithe"—10% given back to God through the church

Many experts claim a budget in which 10 percent of one's income goes to God's work through the church, 10 percent goes into savings, and 80 percent is allocated for living expenses is the hallmark of a balanced Christian financial picture.

EVERYDAY STUFF

2 MAKE A SOUND FINANCIAL PLAN.

Develop a three-to-five-year plan to achieve tithing, and break up the years with meaningful milestones, such as, "5 percent by year two!" Consider three steps that will get you to 10 percent. For longer-term plans, increase your giving by 1 percent of your income each year until you reach 10 percent. Tithing should have an impact on your household budget, but it should not bankrupt you.

3 ESTABLISH YOUR TITHING CHANNELS.

Many tithers give all 10 percent to their home congregation, while others divide it among charities and service organizations that are close to their hearts. Remember that properly placed tithes to reputable organizations are tax-deductible; you'll receive a statement in January of each year. Many congregations send quarterly statements to help keep members on track.

4 CONSIDER MULTIPLE METHODS OF ACCOUNTABILITY TO HELP YOU STAY FOCUSED.

Talk with other members of your congregation about tithing. Making the journey to tithing together can help make it an achievable and meaningful discipline. Consider asking your pastor to pray for your tithing plan.

BE AWARE

] While tithing can be extremely difficult at times, experienced tithers claim the difficult moments are in fact spiritual challenges that have deepened their faith and trust in God.

] Spread the word about tithing quietly with a positive message. If every member of your congregation became a tither, your church could invest heavily in real estate.

] Avoid bragging, boasting, or making others feel inferior when tithing.

] Like tattoos or soap operas, tithing can be habit forming. Most Christians maintain they have never known an ex-tither.

EVERYDAY STUFF

SEVEN COMPLICATED LUTHERAN THEOLOGICAL TERMS IN LATIN AND WHAT THEY MEAN IN PLAIN ENGLISH

Lutheran theologians like to throw around Latin phrases as they argue the finer points of the original "evangelical" theology. This is partly because Latin was the official language of Luther's day and all scholarly writing was done in Latin, and partly because theologians like to sound smarter than you. Memorize the following phrases to impress or alienate your friends.

1 *FACERE QUOD IN SE EST* (FACK-ARRAY KWAHD IN SAY EST), "DO YOUR BEST."
   This is the theological saying that caused Luther so much despair when he was a young monk. If you had to "do your best" in order for God to meet you halfway with grace, Luther wanted to know how could you possibly know when you'd done enough?

2 *JUSTITIA DEI* (YUSS-TITEE-AH DAY-EE), "GOD'S RIGHTEOUSNESS."
   Lutherans believe God *makes* people righteous by grace, through faith, on account of Christ (as revealed in Scripture) as pure gift. This is in contrast to the common idea that you have to exercise some righteousness yourself to earn the gift, whether by being a good person, or making decisions for Jesus, or going to church, or being really sincere, and so on.

3 **THEOLOGIA CRUCIS (TAY-OH-LOH-GEE-AH KREW-KISS), "THEOLOGY OF THE CROSS."**
Luther wrote, "A theologian of glory calls evil good and good evil. A theologian of the cross calls a thing what it actually is." In the end, however, *theologia cruces* hinges on the idea that through the cross, "the Love of God does not find, but creates, that which is pleasing to God."

4 **SERVUM ARBITRIUM (SAIR-WOMB AHR-BEE-TREE-UHM), "BONDAGE OF THE WILL."**
Because of the Fall (original sin) humans are *bound* to reject God's salvation in Christ. God, however, chooses to save rebellious sinners and overrides their will, as it were, making believers out of them. On this point, Luther once confessed that, "God has taken my salvation out of my hands and into his, making it depend on his choice and not mine, and has promised to save me, not by my own work or exertion but by his grace and mercy."

5 **LIBERTATE CHRISTIANI (LEE-BAIR-TAH-TAY KRISS-TEE-AHNNEE), "FREEDOM OF A CHRISTIAN."**
Lutherans like "two-handed thinking" (on the one hand; on the other hand). Luther once wrote that "a Christian is a perfectly free Master, subject to no one," but then in the very next sentence, he wrote, "a Christian is a perfectly dutiful servant, subject to everyone." The point is, both statements are equally true and must be kept in balance.

6 **SIMUL IUSTUS ET PECCATOR (SEE-MUHL EE-YOU-STUSS ET PEE-KAH-TOR), "SAINT AND SINNER AT THE SAME TIME."**
On the one hand, there's the Old You, descended from Adam and Eve, separated from God, rebellious, sinful, cursed, and dying. On the other hand, there's the New You, born of water and the Word, joined to Christ, faithful, righteous, blessed, living now and forever. It's the split personality that began when you were baptized, the one Paul writes about in Romans, chapters 5–8.

7 LEX ET EVANGELIUM (LEKS ET AY-VAN-GAY-LEE-UM), "LAW AND GOSPEL."

There's one phrase that sums it all up for Lutherans: *Lex et Evangelium*. For Lutherans, all of God's word can be discerned in terms of command or promise, or Law and Gospel. For Lutherans, to be a good theologian means being able to tell the difference between Law and Gospel, and speak the Word accordingly.

Honorable mentions include the following:

] ***Adiaphora*** (ah-dee-ah-fore-ah), ***"Indifferent things."*** This term refers to the Lutheran idea that one is free to adopt or not adopt nonessential, that is, human traditions. That includes the tradition of using Latin in theological discussion.

] **Deus absconditus; Deus revelatus** (day-oose ahb-skahndee-toose; day-oose ray-vay-lah-toose), ***"The hidden God"; "The revealed God."*** These terms refer to God's exceptional talent at playing hide-and-go-seek.

] ***Solus Christus*** (soh-loose kree-stoose), ***"Christ alone."*** Collectively known as "the solas," the three terms below reveal Luther's emphasis on each concept as an integrated whole, but together they constitute a pattern of theological thinking that transformed the world. ***Sola gratia*** (soh-lah grah-tee-ah), ***"Grace alone." Sola fide*** (soh-lah fee-day), ***"Faith alone." Sola scriptura*** (soh-lah skreep-too-rah), ***"Scripture alone."***

BE AWARE

] One is *not* required to know Latin to be a Lutheran.

] Using Latin terms in regular conversation may label you as a geek and diminish your chances of ever getting a date or having friends.

HOW TO TELL
THE DIFFERENCE BETWEEN
A "VOCATION"
AND A "VACATION"

Martin Luther's doctrine of vocation is radical because Luther says that a holy *calling* (which is what the word *vocation* means) is not limited to people who are pastors or missionaries. Rather, any job or career is holy when a Christian performs it as part of her or his baptismal call from God to serve others.

A VACATION

EVERYDAY STUFF

1 CONSIDER THE ROLE OF MONEY IN THE CONTEXT OF THE ACTIVITY.

If someone is paying you (however little) rather than making you pay for the opportunity to do the activity, you may be living a vocation, rather than being on vacation.

2 ASSESS THE MEASURE AND TYPE OF FATIGUE THAT RESULTS FROM THE ACTIVITY.

If you are working very hard and getting very tired, but you are not exhausted or downcast, you may be living a vocation rather than being on a vacation. This is a point where vocation and vacation may overlap; discern carefully.

A VOCATION

Vacations and vocations are quite different, as one is recreational and the other is "re-creational"—a life lived through the promises of baptism to participate in God's ongoing work of blessing and redeeming all creation.

3 CHECK NEARBY TABLES FOR BEVERAGES WITH LITTLE UMBRELLAS IN THEM.

If you are serving others rather than being served by others, you may be living a vocation rather than being on vacation. Most employers do not cater to their employees with beverage cart service to their cubicles.

4 DISCERN YOUR IMPACT ON THE PEOPLE AROUND YOU.

If people are genuinely grateful for your presence, rather than just saying so to get a bigger tip, you may be living a vocation rather than being on vacation.

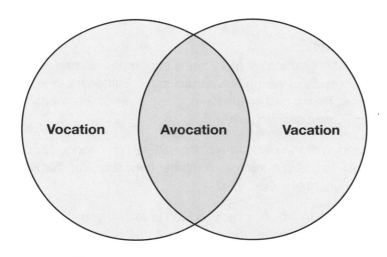

The overlap between one's vocations and one's vacations is called an "avocation," and is usually a hobby of some kind.

EVERYDAY STUFF

5 MEASURE THE LEVEL OF CHALLENGE YOU EXPERIENCE DURING THE ACTIVITY.

If challenged at multiple levels—intellectual, emotional, physical, and spiritual—by what you do each day, you may be living a vocation, rather than being on vacation. While hiking or surfing may be challenging in a physical way, hiking and surfing are probably not vocations for most people.

6 DIFFERENTIATE BETWEEN YOUR LEVEL OF FULFILLMENT AND YOUR LEVEL OF RELAXATION.

If you find fulfillment in what you do beyond mere relaxation and enjoyment, you may be living a vocation, rather than being on vacation.

BE AWARE

] The Lutheran doctrine of vocation encompasses careers and roles outside of workplace employment. Father, mother, sister, brother, friend, and colleague are just a few of the vocations to which Christians are called.

] Vocations of the paid, workplace variety can change. God may choose to call you into many different vocations of this kind during your lifespan.

] Discerning to which vocations God is calling you is among the most important—and ongoing—challenges you face as a Christian.

] The overlap region between vocation and vacation is typically called an *avocation*, which means "a hobby or minor vocation." Avocations show many characteristics of both vocation and vacation, but they have their own name so folks should use it.

HOW TO TELL
THE DIFFERENCE BETWEEN
JUSTICE AND CHARITY

In the Bible, Jesus is most harsh with people who show no concern for those who are hungry, thirsty, without clothes, in prison, and sick. He tells his disciples, "Truly I tell you, just as you did not do it to one of the least of these, you did not do it to me" (Matthew 25:45). Charity and justice are two sides of the same coin—they go together, but they are distinct from each other.

1 CHARITY TYPICALLY INCLUDES PERSONAL INTERACTION THAT RESULTS IN RELIEF.
In the parable of the good Samaritan, the Samaritan provided temporary and immediate relief to someone who was in need. Jesus said, "Go and do likewise" (Luke 10:29-37).

2 JUSTICE USUALLY RELATES TO ACTS THAT ADDRESS UNFAIR SOCIAL, ECONOMIC, OR POLITICAL SYSTEMS.
Moses did not ask Pharaoh for food or supplies for his people, though they certainly needed them. Instead, Moses challenged the oppressive system that imposed suffering and slave labor upon his people. Moses went to the Pharaoh and said, "Let my people go" (Exodus 7:16).

3 **APPLY A DISTINCTION OF EMPHASIS.**

Moses focused on the long-term need of his people rather than the immediate and pressing needs for food and medicine. The good Samaritan's emphasis on charity was on the immediate relief of suffering. Moses' emphasis on justice was directed at the root cause of social injustice. While charity addresses the *symptoms* that are the result of poverty, justice addresses the *systems* that lead to poverty.

4 **FOCUS ON CHARITY IN YOUR DAILY AND WEEKLY LIFE.**

In your local congregation, working at a food bank in your community or volunteering at the local women's shelter is an important work of charity and an important aspect of a Christ-centered life.

5 **CONNECT YOUR EXPERIENCES OF CHARITY WITH A WIDER PERSPECTIVE.**

Find ways to contribute to the elimination of structures that lead to hunger, poverty, or injustice. Consider becoming involved in legislative advocacy, or congregation-based community organizing as a way to address the systems that lead to such oppression.

BE AWARE

] Lutherans tend toward excellence in charity but sometimes slow down a bit when it comes to justice, perhaps because they're uncomfortable being people who rock the boat. This is neither historically nor theologically necessary, as justice is a rudiment to the Lutheran heritage.

] Talk to your pastor or social concerns committee about the important connection and difference between charity and justice. Then find ways in your local congregation to get involved in both.

HOW TO TELL THE DIFFERENCE BETWEEN THE KINGDOM ON THE LEFT AND THE KINGDOM ON THE RIGHT

When Pilate asked Jesus whether he was the king of the Jews, he replied, "My kingdom is not of this world" (John 18:36). This statement has been the starting point of a long series of attempts to define the relationship between Christians and the world. Do Christians have a right to self-defense or civil disobedience? Can they sue their neighbors? Can they serve in the army when God commands us not to kill and Christ commands us to love the enemy? While there is no easy answer to many of these questions, Lutherans tend to favor a set of guiding principles rather than pat answers. Among these principles is Martin Luther's distinction between God's two kingdoms: the earthly or left-handed kingdom, and the heavenly or right-handed kingdom.

This distinction aims to do three things:

] To help Christians live as God's freed and forgiven people in a fallen and sinful world (you don't need to renounce the world and live in a monastery to be holy in God's eyes).

] To clarify that, although God is love and rules the church by love and forgiveness, God uses the force of the law to prevent people from destroying the world and hurting others. At the same time, God uses the law to drive people from one kingdom (on the left) into the other (on the right).

God's Kingdom on the Left	God's Kingdom on the Right

The Lutheran interpretation of God's two kingdoms says they exist in exactly the same place and at exactly the same time, but that God governs differently in each.

] To guide the church in its relationships with the world, especially government, so that Christians understand their main mission to be preaching the gospel to other sinners, as well as their responsibility to speak out against unjust government whenever necessary.

These kingdoms exist in the exact same place, but operate in two distinct ways, or rather, God is the sovereign of the *whole* world and *governs* in two ways:

1. God governs all people in the earthly kingdom through the agency of secular government and the law (by means of force or conviction of sin).

2. Conversely, God rules all people who live by faith in Christ, or those in the spiritual kingdom, with God's right hand, through the gospel (by grace).

Discerning the two kingdoms is quite difficult sometimes and requires a light touch, but it gets easier with practice. Here are some steps to consider.

Kingdom on the Left	Kingdom on the Right
Note the restraint of evil. In the left-hand realm, laws and rules set limits against evildoers and God keeps people from being victimized.	Listen for the sound of mercy. You can trust God's promise of forgiveness of sins and obtain life and salvation.
Seek out institutions that provide safety and security, like families, governments, and the church. God gives structure to your life through them.	Spend time in places where God provides absolution, faithful preaching, and the sacraments of Baptism and Communion.
Look for the places where God provides opportunities for employment, creativity, and social harmony. That's where God is helping life flourish.	Look for sinners who confess that's what they are. You're bound to find them pointing to Jesus as the one who brought them into this realm.
Locate the times and places where sinners come to the end of their ropes. God uses the demands of this kingdom to push them into the other one.	When you find the kingdom on the right, you can be sure the promises God used to bring you there are true.

BE AWARE

] Strictly speaking, neither the term "two kingdoms" nor "two reigns" is used in the Lutheran Confessions, yet both terms have become deeply embedded in Lutheran theology.

] Sinners regularly get the kingdoms confused and try to make each function like the other. Keeping the Ten Commandments and establishing a social order are important on the left, but they're not the same as the kingdom on the right. Any time we try to make our work on the left apply on the right, we deny Christ's work on the cross, which is the only thing that applies there.

] The kingdom on the left needs you to think about how you can participate to promote the well-being of creation. But human reason doesn't work so well in the other kingdom. All you can do there is simply trust that God's promise in the gospel will fully bring in God's will. Only the gospel can truly free people and reorient them to be genuinely concerned for others.

HOW TO TELL IF YOUR WILL IS IN BONDAGE TO SIN AND WHAT TO DO ABOUT IT

Lutherans are among the very few groups that openly, repeatedly, and almost embarrassingly confess that their will is NOT free with respect to sin and salvation and that they, in fact, will wrongly choose sin over faith in Jesus Christ, if given the opportunity. And it is precisely *because* the human will is bound to sin that Christ's death and resurrection are necessary. Still, we forget this from time to time and imagine our wills to be godlike and free.

People whose wills are in bondage to sin exhibit several symptoms. This exercise will help you identify those symptoms:

1 **PERFORM THE FOLLOWING TEST:**
   Using the index and middle fingers of one hand, find your pulse (the wrist, neck, and under the arm are all good places to find your pulse). If a pulse is detected, your will is in bondage. (If no pulse is detected, dial 911. You've got bigger problems than a bound will.)

2 **LOOK FOR THESE SYMPTOMS:**
   - You feel a sense of helplessness and hopelessness after reading the Ten Commandments, like there's no way you can do it.

   - You constantly want more or better stuff, such as clothes, money, electronics, and so on.

   - You occasionally experience envy of persons who have more or better stuff than you.

   - You find it easy to neglect the needs of others in favor of your own needs.

- You do (or desire to do) things you know in your mind you should not do.

- Even at your best you find it impossible to break the cycle and become "good."

3 REORIENT YOUR THINKING TO WHAT THE BIBLE SAYS ABOUT SIN AND HUMAN WILL.

Although many Christians speak of having a "free will," Lutherans believe that human will is bound to sin. As the apostle Paul writes, "For I do not do the good I want, but the evil I do not want is what I do" (Romans 7:19). The necessary remedy lies in Jesus Christ's death and resurrection. If you are not Jesus Christ, you need him.

Confessing in public that your will is bound to sin and that you cannot free yourself will help reorient you toward the One whose will is not bound to sin and who can, in fact, free you.

Once a bound will is identified:

4 ADMIT IT TO YOURSELF.
By admitting that you are in bondage to sin and cannot free yourself you become open to the promises, forgiveness, and surprises of God.

5 CONFESS IT IN PUBLIC.
This is slightly different than admitting it. It is one thing to tell yourself that you're sinful. It is another thing to say it out loud to someone else. Confession means admitting out loud, to someone else or in the company of other sinners, that you are in bondage to sin and in need of Christ.

6 LISTEN ACTIVELY FOR GOD'S PROMISES.
Your confession of sinfulness in worship, to a pastor, or to another Christian should always be followed by words of God's forgiveness. Be confident in God's promise of forgiveness.

7 MOVE FORWARD AS THE NEW ADAM OR NEW EVE THAT CHRIST HAS MADE YOU THROUGH YOUR BAPTISM.
Having admitted and confessed your bondage to sin, and having heard the promises of God, now is time to get over it and get on with living. Even though we are in bondage to sin, God simultaneously gives us the power to be children of God to live a godly life.

8 REPEAT DAILY.
Living in bondage to sin is not easy and requires constant confession and forgiveness.

EVERYDAY STUFF

HOW TO TELL
THE DIFFERENCE BETWEEN
ORIGINAL SIN
AND EVERYDAY SIN

Probably due to the lack of clarity they experience in popular culture and the relative unpleasantness of the subject matter, many Lutherans occasionally commit the minor heresy of confusing *original sin* and *everyday sins*. As with most complex theological issues, the Lutheran method of bringing understanding is to stop and draw a careful distinction.

1   CLARIFY YOUR TERMS.
- Original sin is what many theologians call "the unavoidable desire of humans to disobey God." Original sin is not something that we do; it is something that causes us to do things. It helps to think about original sin as *human sinfulness*.

- Everyday sins are the faithless and stupid things humans do because we are still in the grip of original sin. Everyday sins include things like lying or cheating to get ahead, and intentionally hurting or misusing our bodies or the bodies of others. Everyday sins are sinful *acts*, the kinds of things forbidden in the Ten Commandments.

2   REVISIT THE BASIC RELATIONSHIP BETWEEN CAUSE AND EFFECT.
Original sin is the *reason* that we are tempted to commit everyday sins. In the strange calculus of sin, original sin is the cause; everyday sins are the effects. Put another way, original sin relates to who we *are*; everyday sins relate to what we *do*.

3 SHARPEN THE DISTINCTION TO ITS FINEST POINT.

Original sin and everyday sins are not two different kinds of the same thing. In yet another metaphor, everyday sins are symptoms of the underlying sickness of original sin.

4 LISTEN CAREFULLY TO THE LANGUAGE AROUND THE TERMS; TAKE THEM IN CONTEXT.

If the word *sin* is being used in a way that makes it seem completely *unavoidable*, it is probably being used to mean original sin. For example: "Because of *sin* in the world, there will always be war." On the other hand, if the word *sin* is being used in a way that makes it seem like something you could avoid doing, it is probably being used to mean everyday sin For example: "I am tempted to sin by disobeying my mother."

BE AWARE

] Saying original sin is a cause of your sin, as though "the devil made me do it," does NOT get you off the hook. It's still *your* sin.

] Confusing original sin and everyday sin does not, in itself, qualify as a sin. It's just imperfect judgment.

] While sinfulness and sins are realities in the Christian life, Lutherans know that they are only the last gasps of an enemy that Jesus has defeated forever. Jesus forgives our everyday sins and has freed us finally from the grip of original sin. We are freed and called to be the faithful servants of God we were created to be!

HOW TO TELL THE DIFFERENCE BETWEEN A SINNER AND A SAINT

Many Christians claim they can tell the difference between saints and sinners. Sinners are naughty and do naughty things, they say, and saints are nice and do nice things. For Lutherans, however, who strive to take an honest and searching inventory of human nature, distinguishing saint from sinner has never been easy.

1 GRAPPLE BRIEFLY WITH THE FOLLOWING QUESTION: "CAN THE FINITE BEAR THE INFINITE?"

Originally used by the church to help resolve the debate over whether Jesus was all man (completely human) *or* all God (completely divine), this question can be useful when discerning sinner from saint. Lutherans answer the question by saying, "Yes!" Baptism makes the finite (you) able to bear the infinite (Christ), so it's not a matter of naughty *or* nice, sinner *or* saint (or, in Jesus' case, man *or* God). A person is fully a saint and fully a sinner at the same time.

2 EMBRACE THE SINNER SO THAT THE SAINT CAN BE REVEALED. AVOID PULLING PUNCHES.

Fearlessly and truthfully answer the question, "Am I (or, are you) a sinner?" based strictly on the evidence at hand. (Hint: when in doubt simply measure yourself or the other person against the Ten Commandments.) If you hedge by saying, "No, not totally. I keep some commandments sometimes," you are blissfully deluded.

3   BONE UP ON WHAT THE BIBLE SAYS ABOUT IT.

Scripture makes clear that being a sinner is a prerequisite for being a saint (see Romans 5:8; Galatians 2:17; and Matthew 9:13). Why else would a saint like the apostle Paul "boast" that he was himself the chief of sinners (1 Timothy 1:15)? Why else would he confess that "I do not do the good I want but the evil I do not want is what I do"?

4   EMPLOY STANDARD, LUTHERAN "TWO-HANDED" THINKING.

On the one hand, people are sinners when they disobey God's Commandments and when they doubt or disbelieve the Word of God. The end of such sinners is death. On the other hand, people are saints when they are justified by faith in Christ apart from the works of the law and when they continue to trust and believe God's promises in Christ. The end of such saints is eternal life.

BE AWARE

]   Although Christians are exhorted to "tame the flesh," they can't make themselves "less of a sinner" over time. You can't become, say, 35 percent sinner and 65 percent saint if you just work really hard at it. You can't change the percentages of sinner/saint within you.

]   Traditionally, Lutherans have preferred to use the Latin phrase *simul iustus et peccator*, where *iustus* = "justified one" or "saint" and *peccator* = "sinner." (See "Seven Complicated Lutheran Theological Terms in Latin and What They Mean in Plain English" on page 265.)

HOW TO TELL A SINNER FROM A SAINT

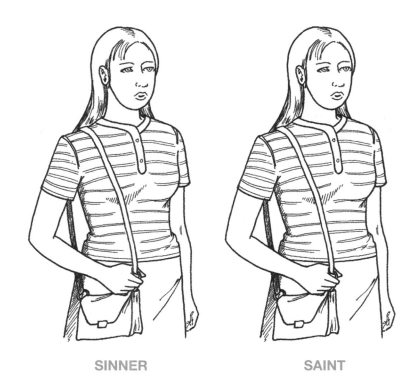

SINNER

SAINT

It's impossible to tell a sinner from a saint, because all people are fully both. The church is filled with them.

HOW TO SHOW THE WORLD YOU'RE A LUTHERAN WITHOUT BEING FLASHY OR BORING

There are dozens of Christian traditions in North America, each emphasizing a slightly different aspect of the Christian faith, and many more people of other faiths. While Lutherans tend toward humility and prefer to avoid the the spotlight, we should not be shy about sharing our Christian faith or our Lutheran way of understanding and living that faith.

Showing the world you're a Lutheran can be accomplished in part by means of a bumper sticker, but this should not represent the totality of your faith expression.

LUTHERANS DO IT WITH GRACE

1 **STRIVE ALWAYS TO SEE THE DIVINE IN THINGS THE WORLD CONSIDERS TO BE MUNDANE, BORING, OR WEAK.**

Lutherans are famous for finding pearls hidden among swine and strength hidden in weakness. Adopting this philosophy equips you with the ability to dethrone worldly powers and proclaim Christ.

2 **CONFESS YOUR FAITH STATUS IN PLAIN LANGUAGE, UNOSTENTATIOUSLY AND WITHOUT FANFARE.**

When talking with someone about faith or religion, simply say, "I am Lutheran," or "I am a Lutheran Christian." (You should be ready to explain what being Lutheran means to you, in case someone asks.)

3 **CONSIDER ADORNING YOURSELF, YOUR HOME, OR YOUR VEHICLE WITH SIMPLE LUTHERAN ACCOUTREMENTS. AVOID GARISH COLORS AND BOLD FONTS WHERE POSSIBLE.**

Wear a Luther's Rose pendant or display the Luther's Rose at your home in the form of a cross-stitched mural, in your office in the form of a paperweight or on your e-mail signature, or on your car in the form of a bumper sticker.

4 **ADOPT A POLICY OF CELEBRATING LIFE EVENTS WITH A NOTE OF SERVICE TO THE NEIGHBOR.**

For a friend or family member's next birthday, make a gift to a Lutheran social service agency (such as Lutheran Disaster Relief or Lutheran Immigration and Refugee Service) in that person's honor. *Note:* Some non-Lutherans may not "get" the value of this kind of celebration; consider also giving that person a gift card to their favorite fast-food restaurant to avoid hurt feelings.

BE AWARE

] Martin Luther wrote that what makes a Christian shoemaker Christian is *not* that he puts crosses on his shoes, but that he makes good shoes. In this way, Luther cautions us that being Christian is not about the signs, symbols, or even the words we use, but about the way we live our lives.

] Many Lutherans live in ways that other Lutherans would call flashy, and vice versa. It's really a matter of perspective.

] Most non-Lutherans automatically associate the word *Lutheran* with the word *boring*. If you err to one side or the other, be flashier rather than more boring.

Martin Luther wrote that what makes a Christian shoemaker Christian is not that he puts crosses on his shoes, but that he makes good shoes. Being Christian is less about the symbols we use to adorn our lives, but the way we live our lives.

HOW TO HANDLE YOURSELF WHEN YOU GET ANGRY AT GOD

While anger may appear to run counter to worshiping God, irritation and even outright anger have been and continue to be legitimate emotions emanating from believers. Appropriate anger may be seen as part of the faithful believer's repertoire of sentiments when used sparingly and within reason.

1 IDENTIFY THE ISSUES.
Directing anger at God serves as a natural response in certain situations, including the sudden death of a loved one or unanswered prayers. However, the source of anger may not always be clear. In such situations, take time, perhaps silently, to identify the basis of your anger.

2 EVALUATE YOUR RESPONSE.
Consider whether your level of hostility compares to what you perceive God's transgression to be. Not getting a raise or failing a test may provoke a generalized sense of anger that includes the Almighty, but nonetheless should be directed elsewhere.

3 WATCH YOUR MOUTH.
Anger is acceptable; disrespect is not. Keep the Commandments at all times. Avoid dishonoring or slandering God.

4 AVOID PHYSICAL VIOLENCE.
Reject taking out anger on other people, places, or things. Wrestling with God has been attempted, but seldom proves fruitful and can lead to hip dislocation and a residual limp. (See Genesis 32:24.)

5 CONSIDER TAKING A TIME-OUT.
Shunning worship is not advised. Use communion time for prayer and continued dialogue with God.

6 REVIEW THE HISTORY OF HUMANS GETTING ANGRY WITH GOD.
You're not the first person to get angry with God, and you won't be the last. Read Scripture to identify how others have worked through "righteous" fury. Note occasional risk of smiting.

7 IDENTIFY AND ACCEPT YOUR OWN RESPONSIBILITY.
Understanding what has caused your anger may lead to introspection and subsequent reassignment of responsibility.

8 MAKE NICE.
At the appropriate time, thank God for steadfastness through times of anger, for forgiving your outburst, and call it a truce.

BE AWARE

] From time to time, anger at God may become nondescript and lingering. Recruiting the counsel of a third party may be wise when anger turns to bitterness. Conversations with a pastor or professional therapist may be valuable. For clergy, such counseling for anger toward God may fall under employee assistant programs under "work-related stress." Check your health-care benefit plan.

EVERYDAY STUFF

HOW TO INVITE A FRIEND OR NEIGHBOR TO CHURCH WITHOUT TERRIFYING THEM

Introverted and unostentatious by nature, Lutherans are often reserved in expressing their personal faith to others. Many fear that extending invitations to attend church may permanently scare off friends and neighbors or get them labeled as "Jesus freaks." Employing a natural and comfortable approach when inviting others, however, can ease this fear for everyone.

Sunday School Christmas program

newcomers to church

Regular church worship services can be too intimidating for some newcomers. Consider inviting them instead to a special event so they can "warm up" to the idea of church.

1 **WORK CONSISTENTLY TO DEVELOP OPEN RELATIONSHIPS WITH FRIENDS AND NEIGHBORS.**
While this may seem obvious, when it comes to an evangelistic lifestyle, an invitation to church is less likely to frighten those who know you well. An invitation to church may also be a way to deepen a relationship with a new acquaintance, too.

2 **FIND A COMFORTABLE, PERSONAL LANGUAGE WHEN YOU TALK ABOUT YOUR CHURCH; SHARE EXPERIENCES; AVOID USING CLICHÉS YOU'VE LEARNED FROM POPULAR CULTURE.**
Talk about people and events at your church as though they were a natural part of your life; and wouldn't it be nice if they actually were? If you had an uplifting experience during a worship service, share it. This may intrigue your friends and encourage them to ask questions.

3 **MAKE IT A PRACTICE TO TALK FREQUENTLY ABOUT YOUR FAITH. USE "I" STATEMENTS.**
Share with your friends and neighbors why active participation in a community of faith is important to you. Talk about sermons that you find thought provoking and Bible studies where you learned something new. Putting these anecdotes in terms of your own experience can help avoid making others feel foisted upon.

4 **CONSIDER DOING A LITTLE FOISTING ONCE IN A WHILE.**
On rare occasions, the best move is gently to connect friends with your church through kindly force or coercion. For example, "kidnap" your friend on a Sunday morning and take him or her to church when your original invitation was "just for coffee." Or "just drop by" the church picnic on your way to the ballgame.

5 **MAKE SIMPLE, EVERYDAY CONNECTIONS BETWEEN FAITH AND DAILY LIVING.**

Explain the relationship you see between your faith and your daily living. How does attending church prepare you for the week ahead (or liberate you from the week behind)? Ask if they would like to share this experience.

6 **USE SPECIAL EVENTS AS UNIQUE OPPORTUNITIES.**

"Regular church" can be too intimidating for some. Consider inviting friends and neighbors to a congregational special musical event such as the Christmas pageant, for example. Invite them to special dinners. Eating is both a necessary and nonthreatening activity. Ask them to join you on a mission trip or to help at the food bank.

7 **ENCOURAGE THE CHILDREN IN YOUR LIFE TO INVITE FRIENDS.**

Young children and youth are often less threatening than adults and can be used quite shamelessly in service to the gospel. Encourage your children to invite their friends to church programs and worship services. Make it a condition of Saturday-night sleepovers that the whole household attends church the next day. This can lead to families attending together.

BE AWARE

] Teaching yourself to accentuate the positive about your church
   will almost certainly have salutary effects on your evangelistic
   lifestyle.

] Complaining about people at your church is a poor reflection
   of both you and your church, and it will ultimately create
   greater terror in those whom you would invite.

] Words such as *witness, proselytize, testimony,* and *evangelism* can cause shaky knees and faint hearts among many
   un-churched, de-churched, or semi-churched persons. Use
   extreme caution when employing them in invitations.

EVERYDAY STUFF

SMALL CATECHISM OF MARTIN LUTHER

As printed in *Evangelical Lutheran Worship*

THE TEN COMMANDMENTS

The First Commandment

You shall have no other gods.

What is this? or *What does this mean?*
We are to fear, love, and trust God above all things.

The Second Commandment

You shall not make wrongful use of the name of the Lord your God.

What is this? or *What does this mean?*
We are to fear and love God, so that we do not curse, swear, practice magic, lie, or deceive using God's name, but instead use that very name in every time of need to call on, pray to, praise, and give thanks to God.

The Third Commandment

Remember the sabbath day, and keep it holy.

What is this? or *What does this mean?*
We are to fear and love God, so that we do not despise preaching or God's word, but instead keep that word holy and gladly hear and learn it.

The Fourth Commandment

Honor your father and your mother.

What is this? or *What does this mean?*
We are to fear and love God, so that we neither despise nor anger our parents and others in authority, but instead honor, serve, obey, love, and respect them.

The Fifth Commandment

You shall not murder.

What is this? or *What does this mean?*
We are to fear and love God, so that we neither endanger nor harm the lives of our neighbors, but instead help and support them in all of life's needs.

The Sixth Commandment

You shall not commit adultery.

What is this? or *What does this mean?*
We are to fear and love God, so that we lead pure and decent lives in word and deed, and each of us loves and honors his or her spouse.

The Seventh Commandment

You shall not steal.

What is this? or *What does this mean?*
We are to fear and love God, so that we neither take our neighbors' money or property nor acquire them by using shoddy merchandise or crooked deals, but instead help them to improve and protect their property and income.

The Eighth Commandment

You shall not bear false witness against your neighbor.

What is this? or *What does this mean?*
We are to fear and love God, so that we do not tell lies about our neighbors, betray or slander them, or destroy their reputations. Instead we are to come to their defense, speak well of them, and interpret everything they do in the best possible light.

The Ninth Commandment

You shall not covet your neighbor's house.

What is this? or *What does this mean?*
We are to fear and love God, so that we do not try to trick our neighbors out of their inheritance or property or try to get it for ourselves by claiming to have a legal right to it and the like, but instead be of help and service to them in keeping what is theirs.

The Tenth Commandment

You shall not covet your neighbor's wife, or male or female slave, or ox, or donkey, or anything that belongs to your neighbor.

What is this? or *What does this mean?*
We are to fear and love God, so that we do not entice, force, or steal away from our neighbors their spouses, household workers, or livestock, but instead urge them to stay and fulfill their responsibilities to our neighbors.

What then does God say about all these commandments?
God says the following: "I, the Lord your God, am a jealous God, punishing children for the iniquity of parents, to the third and the fourth generation of those who reject me, but showing steadfast love to the thousandth generation of those who love me and keep my commandments."

What is this? or *What does this mean?*
God threatens to punish all who break these commandments. Therefore we are to fear his wrath and not disobey these commandments. However, God promises grace and every good thing to all those who keep these commandments. Therefore we also are to love and trust him and gladly act according to his commands.

THE CREED

The First Article: On Creation

I believe in God, the Father almighty, creator of heaven and earth.

What is this? or *What does this mean?*
I believe that God has created me together with all that exists. God has given me and still preserves my body and soul: eyes, ears, and all limbs and senses; reason and all mental faculties.

In addition, God daily and abundantly provides shoes and clothing, food and drink, house and farm, spouse and children, fields, livestock, and all property—along with all the necessities and nourishment for this body and life. God protects me against all danger and shields and preserves me from all evil. And all this is done out of pure, fatherly, and divine goodness and mercy, without any merit or worthiness of mine at all! For all of this I owe it to God to thank and praise, serve and obey him. This is most certainly true.

The Second Article: On Redemption

I believe in Jesus Christ, God's only Son, our Lord, who was conceived by the Holy Spirit, born of the virgin Mary, suffered under Pontius Pilate, was crucified, died, and was buried; he descended to the dead.* On the third day he rose again; he ascended into heaven, he is seated at the right hand of the Father, and he will come to judge the living and the dead.

*Or, "he descended into hell," another translation of this text in widespread use.

What is this? or *What does this mean?*
I believe that Jesus Christ, true God, begotten of the Father in eternity, and also a true human being, born of the virgin Mary, is my Lord. He has redeemed me, a lost and condemned human being. He has purchased and freed me from all sins, from death, and from the power of the devil, not with gold or silver but with his holy, precious blood and with his innocent suffering and death. He has done all this in order that I may belong to him, live under him in his kingdom, and serve him in eternal righteousness, innocence, and blessedness, just as he is risen from the dead and lives and rules eternally. This is most certainly true.

The Third Article: On Being Made Holy

I believe in the Holy Spirit, the holy catholic church, the communion of saints, the forgiveness of sins, the resurrection of the body, and the life everlasting.

What is this? or *What does this mean?*
I believe that by my own understanding or strength I cannot believe in Jesus Christ my Lord or come to him, but instead the Holy Spirit has called me through the gospel, enlightened me with his gifts, made me holy and kept me in the true faith, just as he calls, gathers, enlightens, and makes holy the whole Christian church on earth and keeps it with Jesus Christ in the one common, true faith. Daily in this Christian church the Holy Spirit abundantly forgives all sins—mine and those of all believers. On the last day the Holy Spirit will raise me and all the dead and will give to me and all believers in Christ eternal life. This is most certainly true.

THE LORD'S PRAYER

Our Father in heaven.

What is this? or *What does this mean?*
With these words God wants to attract us, so that we come to believe he is truly our Father and we are truly his children, in order that we may ask him boldly and with complete confidence, just as loving children ask their loving father.

Hallowed be your name.

What is this? or *What does this mean?*
It is true that God's name is holy in itself, but we ask in this prayer that it may also become holy in and among us.

How does this come about?
Whenever the word of God is taught clearly and purely and we, as God's children, also live holy lives according to it. To this end help us, dear Father in heaven! However, whoever teaches and lives otherwise than the word of God teaches, dishonors the name of God among us. Preserve us from this, heavenly Father!

Your kingdom come.

What is this? or *What does this mean?*
In fact, God's kingdom comes on its own without our prayer, but we ask in this prayer that it may also come to us.

How does this come about?
Whenever our heavenly Father gives us his Holy Spirit, so that through the Holy Spirit's grace we believe God's holy word and live godly lives here in time and hereafter in eternity.

The Third Petition

Your will be done, on earth as in heaven.

What is this? or *What does this mean?*
In fact, God's good and gracious will comes about without our prayer, but we ask in this prayer that it may also come about in and among us.

How does this come about?
Whenever God breaks and hinders every evil scheme and will—as are present in the will of the devil, the world, and our flesh—that would not allow us to hallow God's name and would prevent the coming of his kingdom, and instead whenever God strengthens us and keeps us steadfast in his word and in faith until the end of our lives. This is God's gracious and good will.

The Fourth Petition

Give us today our daily bread.

What is this? or *What does this mean?*
In fact, God gives daily bread without our prayer, even to all evil people, but we ask in this prayer that God cause us to recognize what our daily bread is and to receive it with thanksgiving.

What then does "daily bread" mean?
Everything included in the necessities and nourishment for our bodies, such as food, drink, clothing, shoes, house, farm, fields, livestock, money, property, an upright spouse,

upright children, upright members of the household, upright and faithful rulers, good government, good weather, peace, health, decency, honor, good friends, faithful neighbors, and the like.

The Fifth Petition

Forgive us our sins, as we forgive those who sin against us.

What is this? or *What does this mean?*
We ask in this prayer that our heavenly Father would not regard our sins nor deny these petitions on their account, for we are worthy of nothing for which we ask, nor have we earned it. Instead we ask that God would give us all things by grace, for we daily sin much and indeed deserve only punishment. So, on the other hand, we, too, truly want to forgive heartily and to do good gladly to those who sin against us.

The Sixth Petition

Save us from the time of trial.

What is this? or *What does this mean?*
It is true that God tempts no one, but we ask in this prayer that God would preserve and keep us, so that the devil, the world, and our flesh may not deceive us or mislead us into false belief, despair, and other great and shameful sins, and that, although we may be attacked by them, we may finally prevail and gain the victory.

The Seventh Petition

And deliver us from evil.

What is this? or *What does this mean?*
We ask in this prayer, as in a summary, that our Father in heaven may deliver us from all kinds of evil—affecting body or soul, property or reputation—and at last, when our final hour comes, may grant us a blessed end and take us by grace from this valley of tears to himself in heaven.

Conclusion

[For the kingdom, the power, and the glory are yours, now and forever.] Amen.

What is this? or *What does this mean?*
That I should be certain that such petitions are acceptable to and heard by our Father in heaven, for he himself commanded us to pray like this and has promised to hear us. "Amen, amen" means "Yes, yes, it is going to come about just like this."

THE SACRAMENT OF HOLY BAPTISM

I

What is baptism?
Baptism is not simply plain water. Instead, it is water used according to God's command and connected with God's word.

What then is this word of God?
Where our Lord Christ says in Matthew 28, "Go therefore and make disciples of all nations, baptizing them in the name of the Father and of the Son and of the Holy Spirit."

II

What gifts or benefits does baptism grant?
It brings about forgiveness of sins, redeems from death and the devil, and gives eternal salvation to all who believe it, as the words and promise of God declare.

What are these words and promise of God?
Where our Lord Christ says in Mark 16, "The one who believes and is baptized will be saved; but the one who does not believe will be condemned."

III

How can water do such great things?
Clearly the water does not do it, but the word of God, which is with and alongside the water, and faith, which trusts this word of God in the water. For without the word of God the water is plain water and not a baptism, but with the word of God it is a baptism, that is, a grace-filled water of life and a "bath of the new birth in the Holy Spirit," as St. Paul says to Titus in chapter 3, "through the water of rebirth and renewal by the Holy Spirit. This Spirit he poured out on us richly through Jesus Christ our Savior, so that, having been justified by his grace, we might become heirs according to the hope of eternal life. The saying is sure."

What then is the significance of such a baptism with water?
It signifies that the old person in us with all sins and evil desires is to be drowned and die through daily sorrow for sin and through repentance, and on the other hand that daily a new person is to come forth and rise up to live before God in righteousness and purity forever.

Where is this written?
St. Paul says in Romans 6, "We have been buried with Christ by baptism into death, so that, just as Christ was raised from the dead by the glory of the Father, so we too might walk in newness of life."

How people are to be taught to confess

What is confession?
Confession consists of two parts. One is that we confess our sins. The other is that we receive the absolution, that is, forgiveness, from the pastor as from God himself and by no means doubt but firmly believe that our sins are thereby forgiven before God in heaven.

Which sins is a person to confess?
Before God one is to acknowledge the guilt for all sins, even those of which we are not aware, as we do in the Lord's Prayer. However, before the pastor we are to confess only those sins of which we have knowledge and which trouble us.

Which sins are these?
Here reflect on your place in life in light of the Ten Commandments: whether you are father, mother, son, daughter, master, mistress, servant; whether you have been disobedient, unfaithful, lazy, whether you have harmed anyone by word or deed; whether you have stolen, neglected, wasted, or injured anything.

THE SACRAMENT OF THE ALTAR

What is the Sacrament of the Altar?
It is the true body and blood of our Lord Jesus Christ under the bread and wine, instituted by Christ himself for us Christians to eat and to drink.

Where is this written?
The holy evangelists Matthew, Mark, and Luke, and St. Paul write thus:

"In the night in which he was betrayed, our Lord Jesus took bread, and gave thanks; broke it, and gave it to his disciples, saying: Take and eat; this is my body, given for you. Do this for the remembrance of me. Again, after supper, he took the cup, gave thanks, and gave it for all to drink, saying: This cup is the new covenant in my blood, shed for you and for all people for the forgiveness of sin. Do this for the remembrance of me."

What is the benefit of such eating and drinking?
The words "given for you" and "shed for you for the forgiveness of sin" show us that forgiveness of sin, life, and salvation are given to us in the sacrament through these words, because where there is forgiveness of sin, there is also life and salvation.

How can bodily eating and drinking do such a great thing?
Eating and drinking certainly do not do it, but rather the words that are recorded: "given for you" and "shed for you for the forgiveness of sin." These words, when accompanied by the physical eating and drinking, are the essential thing in the sacrament, and whoever believes these very words has what they declare and state, namely, "forgiveness of sin."

Who, then, receives this sacrament worthily?
Fasting and bodily preparation are in fact a fine external discipline, but a person who has faith in these words, "given for you" and "shed for you for the forgiveness of sin," is really worthy and well prepared. However, a person who does not believe these words or doubts them is unworthy and unprepared, because the words "for you" require truly believing hearts.

THE MORNING BLESSING

In the morning, as soon as you get out of bed, you are to make the sign of the holy cross and say: "God the Father, Son, and Holy Spirit watch over me. Amen."

Then, kneeling or standing, say the Apostles' Creed and the Lord's Prayer. If you wish, you may in addition recite this little prayer as well: "I give thanks to you, heavenly Father, through Jesus Christ your dear Son, that you have protected me through the night from all harm and danger. I ask that you would also protect me today from sin and all evil, so that my life and actions may please you. Into your hands I commend myself: my body, my soul, and all that is mine. Let your holy angel be with me, so that the wicked foe may have no power over me. Amen."

After singing a hymn perhaps (for example, one on the Ten Commandments) or whatever else may serve your devotion, you are to go to your work joyfully.

THE EVENING BLESSING

In the evening, when you go to bed, you are to make the sign of the holy cross and say: "God the Father, Son, and Holy Spirit watch over me. Amen."

Then, kneeling or standing, say the Apostles' Creed and the Lord's Prayer. If you wish, you may in addition recite this little prayer as well: "I give thanks to you, heavenly Father, through Jesus Christ your dear Son, that you have graciously protected me today. I ask you to forgive me all my sins, where I have done wrong, and graciously to protect me tonight. Into your hands I commend myself: my body, my soul, and all that is mine. Let your holy angel be with me, so that the wicked foe may have no power over me. Amen."

Then you are to go to sleep quickly and cheerfully.

TABLE BLESSINGS

The children and the members of the household are to come devoutly to the table, fold their hands, and recite: "The eyes of all wait upon you, O Lord, and you give them their food in due season. You open your hand and satisfy the desire of every living creature."

Then they are to recite the Lord's Prayer and the following prayer: "Lord God, heavenly Father, bless us and these your gifts, which we receive from your bountiful goodness, through Jesus Christ our Lord. Amen."

Similarly, after eating they should in the same manner fold their hands and recite devoutly: "Give thanks to the Lord, for the Lord is good, for God's mercy endures forever. God provides food for the cattle and for the young ravens when they cry. God is not impressed by the might of a horse, and has no pleasure in the speed of a runner, but finds pleasure in those who fear the Lord, in those who await God's steadfast love."

Then recite the Lord's Prayer and the following prayer: "We give thanks to you, Lord God our Father, through Jesus Christ our Lord for all your benefits, you who live and reign forever. Amen."

GLOSSARY OF LUTHERAN WORSHIP TERMS

acolyte From the Greek for "to follow"; a lay liturgical assistant (often but not necessarily a youth) who serves in such various roles as crucifer, torchbearer, banner-bearer, bookbearer, candlelighter, and server.

Advent From the Latin for "coming"; the four weeks before Christmas which constitute the first season of the liturgical year.

Advent wreath A wreath with four candles, used during the four weeks of Advent.

Affirmation of Baptism Rite used for confirmation, reception of new members, and restoration to membership.

alb Full-length white vestment used in worship since the sixth century; usually worn with cincture. Worn by presiding and assisting ministers, acolytes, choristers.

altar Table in the chancel used for the celebration of the Holy Communion. It is the central furnishing of the worship space.

altar rail Railing enclosing the chancel at which people stand or kneel to receive Holy Communion.

ambo Another (more historic) name for the pulpit, reading desk, or lectern.

ante-communion That portion of the Holy Communion liturgy preceding the great thanksgiving.

antependium Parament for pulpit and lectern.

apse The semicircular (or polygonal) projection or alcove at the end of the chancel in traditional church architecture.

Ascension Principal festival occurring 40 days after Easter Day, celebrating Christ's ascension to heaven.

ashes Symbol of repentance and mortality used in the Ash Wednesday liturgy; made by burning palms from previous year.

Ash Wednesday First day of Lent; occurs between February 4 and March 10. Name derives from the traditional practice of imposing ashes on worshipers' foreheads.

assisting minister Lay person who assists the ordained presiding minister in worship leadership.

baptism The sacrament of water and the Holy Spirit, in which we are joined to Christ's death and resurrection and initiated into the church.

baptistery The area in which the baptismal font is located.

Benedicite, omnia opera (benn-eh-DEECH-ih-tay, OHMnee-ah OH-purr-ah) Latin title for the final canticle in the Easter Vigil, "All you works of the Lord, bless the Lord," from Song of the Three Young Men.

Benedictus (benn-eh-DIKtus) Latin title for the gospel canticle "Blessed be the God of Israel," in Morning Prayer, from Luke 1:68-79.

black Liturgical color for Ash Wednesday; symbolizes ashes, repentance, and humiliation.

blue Liturgical color for Advent; symbolizes hope.

burse Square fabric-covered case in which the communion linens are often carried to and from the altar.

candlelighter Long-handled device used to light and extinguish candles.

candlestick Ornamental base holder for candle.

cassock Full-length black "undergarment" worn under surplice or cotta.

catechumen A person (usually an adult or older youth) preparing for Holy Baptism through a process of formation and special rites leading up to baptism at the Easter Vigil.

catechumenate The process for preparing adults and older youth for Holy Baptism, often culminating at the Easter Vigil. It is a process of growth in spirituality, worship, service, as well as learning, and is based on the practice of the early church.

censer Vessel in which incense is burned; also called thurible.

chalice Cup used for the wine in the Holy Communion.

chancel Elevated area where altar and pulpit/ambo are located.

chasuble (CHAH-zuh-bel) The principal vestment for the Holy Communion liturgy; worn like a poncho by the presiding minister over alb and stole.

chrism (krizm) From the Greek for "Anointed One," a title for Christ.

Fragrant oil used for anointing in Holy Baptism.

chrismon (KRIZ-mohn) From the words "Christ monograms"; symbols of Christ often used to decorate Christmas trees.

Christ the King The last Sunday of the church year, celebrating the kingship or sovereignty of Christ.

Christmas Principal festival of the church year which celebrates Christ's birth or nativity; also known as the Nativity of Our Lord.

ciborium (sih-BOR-ee-um) Tall covered vessel which holds wafers for the Holy Communion.

cincture (SINK-chur) Rope belt worn with an alb.

columbarium (KOLL-um-BARR-ee-um) Wall or other structure with niches for burial of ashes from cremation.

Compline (KAHM-plin) From the Latin for "complete," referring to the prayers which complete the day's worship. An order for night prayer used as the last worship service before bed. Also known as Prayer at the Close of the Day.

confirmation Liturgical form of Affirmation of Baptism, marking the completion of a period of instruction in the Christian faith. Used with youth who were baptized as infants.

cope Long cape worn by worship leader, lay or ordained, for certain processions and ceremonial occasions.

corporal Square white linen cloth placed on the center of the fair linen on the mensa, on which the eucharistic vessels are placed for the celebration of Holy Communion.

corpus Latin for "body." Carved figure of Christ attached to a cross; together, cross and corpus are a crucifix.

cotta (KOTT-ah) Short white vestment worn over cassock by acolytes and choir members (unless albs are worn).

credence (KREE-dentz) Shelf or table at chancel wall which holds sacramental vessels and offering plates.

crosier (KROH-zher) Crook-shaped staff often carried by a bishop in his/her own synod as a sign of shepherding authority.

crucifer The lay assisting minister or senior acolyte who carries the processional cross or crucifix.

crucifix Cross with a corpus attached.

cruet Glass vessel containing wine for the Holy Communion, oil for anointing, or water for the lavabo.

A cruet

daily prayer The daily services of readings and prayer, including Morning Prayer (Matins), Evening Prayer (Vespers), and Night Prayer (Compline).

dossal Fabric hanging behind and above traditional east-wall altar.

east wall The wall behind the altar, regardless of whether the wall is geographically to the east.

eastwall altar An altar attached to the wall.

Easter Principal festival of the church year which celebrates Christ's resurrection. Easter Day (which occurs between March 22 and April 25) is known as the Resurrection of Our Lord and as the "queen of feasts." The Easter season lasts for 50 days, a "week of weeks."

Easter Vigil Festive liturgy on Easter Eve that includes the lighting of the new fire and procession of the paschal candle, readings from Scripture, Holy Baptism with the renewal of baptismal vows, and Holy Communion.

elements The earthly elements used in the celebration of the sacraments: bread and wine in Holy Communion, and water in Holy Baptism.

Epiphany Principal festival celebrated on January 6, marking the visit of the magi to Jesus and the consequent revelation of Christ to the world.

eucharist (YOO-kar-ist) From the Greek for "thanksgiving"; a name for the Holy Communion. The sacrament of Word, bread, and wine (in which the two earthly elements constitute the body and blood of our Lord) for which we give thanks, and through which we are nourished and strengthened in Christ's name and sustained in baptismal unity in him.

Fraction of the bread in
Holy Communion

Evening Prayer An evening worship service of scripture readings and prayer; also known as Vespers.

ewer (YOO-er) A pitcher used for carrying water to the baptismal font.

fair linen Top white linen cloth covering the mensa of the altar and thus serving as the table cloth for the Lord's Supper.

flagon (FLAG-un) Pitcher-like vessel from which wine is poured into the chalice for the Holy Communion.

font From the Latin for "fountain"; the pool or basin which holds water for Holy Baptism.

fraction Ceremonial breaking of the bread in the Holy Communion liturgy.

free-standing altar An altar which is not attached to the wall, and behind which the ministers stand (facing the congregation) for the celebration of Holy Communion.

frontal Parament that covers the entire front of the altar, from the top edge of the mensa down to the floor; *see also* Laudian frontal.

funeral pall Large white cloth cover placed on the coffin when brought into the nave for the burial liturgy. If an urn is used for ashes, a small white cloth is used to cover it.

gold Liturgical color for Easter Day, giving special prominence to this single most important festival of the year.

Good Friday The Friday in Holy Week that observes Christ's crucifixion and death. The chancel and altar are bare of all appointments, paraments, and linens.

Greek cross Ancient form of the cross in which the four arms are of equal length.

green Liturgical color for the non-festival seasons after Pentecost and Epiphany; symbolic of growth in the Christian way of life.

Holy Trinity The First Sunday after Pentecost, which celebrates the doctrine of the Trinity (one God in three persons: Father, Son, and Holy Spirit).

Holy Week The week between the Sunday of the Passion (Palm Sunday) and Easter, which recalls the events of the last days of Christ's life.

host Wafer, made of unleavened bread, for the Holy Communion.

host box Short, round, covered container which holds the supply of hosts for the Holy Communion. Also known as pyx.

incense Mixture of resins for ceremonial burning, symbolic of our prayers rising to God (see Psalm 141); one of the gifts of the magi to Jesus on the Epiphany.

Incense

intinction From the Latin for "to dip"; the practice of administering the eucharistic elements by dipping the host into the wine; does not work well with whole bread.

Laudian frontal A type of frontal which entirely covers the top and all sides (to the floor) of a free-standing altar.

lavabo bowl (lah-VAH-boh) Bowl used for the act of cleansing the presiding minister's hands (this act is known as the lavabo) in the Holy Communion or after the imposition of ashes or oil.

lectern Reading stand in the chancel from which the scripture readings may be proclaimed.

lectionary The appointed system of scripture readings for the days of the church year. Also refers to the book that contains these readings.

lector A lay assisting minister who reads the first and second readings from Scripture in the Holy Communion liturgy, or the biblical readings in other rites.

Lent From the Anglo-Saxon for "spring"; the penitential 40-day season (excluding Sundays) before Easter, beginning with Ash Wednesday. Symbolic of Christ's 40 days in the wilderness. Lent is traditionally the season when candidates prepare for Holy Baptism, which is celebrated at the Easter Vigil.

lenten veil Cloth used to cover crosses, sculpture, pictures, and other objects during Lent.

linens Refers to three groups of white linen cloths: altar linens (cerecloth, protector linen, and fair linen), communion linens (corporal, pall, purificators, and veil), and other linens (credence linen, offertory table linen, lavabo towel, and baptismal towel).

liturgy From the Greek for "the people's work"; the prescribed worship service of the church.

Magnificat (mahg-NIFF-ihkaht) Latin title for the canticle, "My soul proclaims the greatness of the Lord," which is the gospel canticle in Evening Prayer, and is from Luke 1:46-55.

Matins (MAT-ins) From the Latin for "morning"; morning service of scripture reading and prayer; also known as Morning Prayer.

Maundy Thursday (MAWNdee) From the Latin mandatum for "commandment"; the Thursday in Holy Week which commemorates the institution of the Holy Communion at the Last Supper, during which Jesus commanded his disciples to love one another.

memorial garden Usually a courtyard garden on church property in which ashes are mixed with the soil for interment after cremation.

mensa From the Latin for "table"; the top surface of the altar.

missal Altar service book.

missal stand Stand or cushion on the altar on which the altar service book is placed during the Holy Communion liturgy.

miter (MY-ter) From the Greek for "turban." A liturgical hat worn by a bishop.

Morning Prayer Morning service of scripture reading and prayer; also known as Matins.

narthex Entrance hall and gathering space of a church building which leads to the nave.

nave From the Latin for "ship"; the section of the church building between the narthex and the chancel, where the congregation assembles for worship.

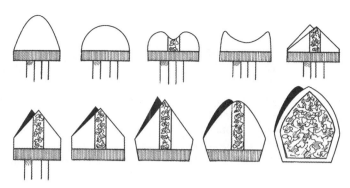

Miters go on top of bishops. They've been wearing them a long time.

new fire The fire kindled on Easter Eve, used to light the paschal candle for the Easter Vigil. Symbolic of Christ's resurrected presence.

Nunc dimittis (NOONK dih-MIH-tiss) Latin title for the canticle from Luke 2:29-32, "Now, Lord, you let your servant go in peace," used in Night Prayer and as a song after Holy Communion.

occasional service Liturgical rite used from time to time, including rites for burial, marriage, healing, ordination, dedication of a church building, installation of a pastor, confirmation (Affirmation of Baptism), and so forth.

ordinary Those parts of the eucharistic liturgy which do not change from week to week.

orphrey (OR-free) From the Latin for "gold." Ornamental band on a chasuble or parament.

ossuary Small container holding the remains after a cremation.

pall Linen-covered square placed over rim of the chalice. (*See also* funeral pall.)

Palm Sunday *See* Sunday of the Passion.

paraments Cloth hangings of various seasonal liturgical colors used to adorn the altar and pulpit/ambo/lectern.

paschal candle Large white candle carried in procession during the Easter Vigil, placed near the altar and lighted during the Easter season, symbolizing Christ's resurrected presence. At other times of the year, it is placed near the font and lighted for Holy Baptism, and placed at the head of the coffin and lighted for the burial liturgy.

paten (PATT-en) Plate used to hold bread or hosts during the Holy Communion liturgy.

Paschal candle

pectoral cross A cross on a chain, worn around the neck by a bishop.

Pentecost From the Greek for "fiftieth day"; principal festival of the church year, occurring 50 days after Easter. Celebrates the descent of the Holy Spirit to the crowd gathered in Jerusalem.

317

Phos hilaron (FOHS HILL-uhron) Greek for "light of glory"; hence, the Greek name for the canticle in Evening Prayer which begins "Joyous light of glory."

piscina A special drain in the sacristy which goes directly into the ground, used for disposal of baptismal water and wine remaining in the chalice after the Holy Communion.

Prayer at the Close of the Day Night prayer service used as the last worship before retiring for the night. Also known as Compline or Night Prayer.

presiding minister The ordained pastor who presides at a worship service.

prie-dieu (pree-DYOO) French term for "prayer desk"; used in the chancel for daily prayer services, confirmation, and weddings, as well as by ministers at other times when kneeling for prayer is desired.

processional cross A cross or crucifix on a tall staff used to lead processions.

processional torch See torch.

propers The varying portions of the communion service which are appointed for each day (or season) of the church year; include the prayer of the day, psalm, readings, gospel acclamation, and proper preface.

protector linen White linen cloth placed on the mensa between

Processional cross

the cerecloth and the fair linen, to which the parament may be attached.

pulpit Raised reading desk in the chancel from which the gospel is read and the sermon preached. See also ambo.

purificator Square linen napkin used to cleanse the rim of the chalice during the distribution of Holy Communion.

purple Liturgical color for Lent, symbolizing penitence.

pyx (PIKS) See host box.

red Bright red liturgical color, symbolic of the fire of the Holy Spirit. Used on the Day of Pentecost, Reformation Day, martyrs' days, and on major church occasions such as ordination, the dedication of a church building, church anniversaries, and synod/churchwide assemblies.

reredos (RAIR-eh-doss) Carved stone or wood panel behind and above an eastwall altar.

Responsive Prayer Brief liturgical order of versicles and responses.

retable (REE-tay-bel) A step or shelf at the rear of the mensa of an eastwall altar, on which cross, candlesticks, and flowers are placed. Also known as a gradine.

rite The text and ceremonies of a liturgical worship service.

rubric From the Latin for "red"; a direction for the proper conduct of a worship service. Rubrics are usually printed in red.

sacrament A rite commanded by Christ that uses an earthly element with the word of God to convey God's grace; Holy Baptism and Holy Communion.

sacristy A room used for storage and preparation of items needed in worship; also used for vesting before services.

sanctuary The section of the chancel that immediately surrounds the altar.

sanctuary lamp A constantly burning candle sometimes suspended from the ceiling or mounted on the chancel wall; in Roman Catholic and some Episcopal churches, symbolizes the reserved sacrament.

Sanctuary lamp, bronze hanging

scarlet The deep red liturgical color used from the Sunday of the Passion (Palm Sunday) through Maundy Thursday. Symbolic of the blood of the passion of Christ.

sign of the cross Gesture of tracing the outline of the cross with the hand, as a mark of belonging to Christ in Holy Baptism (during which it is first placed on one's forehead).

spoon Perforated utensil sometimes used to remove foreign particles from wine in the chalice. A spoon is also used with the granular incense.

stole Cloth band in liturgical color worn over the alb or surplice around a pastor's neck and hanging to the knees. Signifies ordination and the yoke of obedience to Christ.

stripping of the altar Ceremony at the conclusion of the Maundy Thursday liturgy, in which all appointments, linens, and paraments are removed from the altar and chancel in preparation for Good Friday.

Sunday of the Passion The first day of Holy Week, also known as Palm Sunday. Commemorates both Christ's triumphant entry into Jerusalem and his crucifixion.

superfrontal Short parament that hangs over the front of the mensa of an eastwall altar; now rarely used.

surplice White vestment worn over the cassock; used especially for daily prayer services.

Te Deum laudamus (tay DAYum lau-DAH-moos) Latin for "We praise you, God"; a title for the canticle used in Morning Prayer.

Tenebrae (TENN-eh-bray) From the Latin for "shadows"; a service sometimes used evenings during Holy Week, in which candles on a Tenebrae candle hearse.

thurible Vessel in which incense is burned; also known as a censer.

thurifer The person who cares the thurible.

torch Large candle on a staff carried in processions, often flanking

Torch

the processional cross or gospel book.

torchbearer An acolyte who carries a processional torch.

Transfiguration Festival celebrated on the last Sunday after the Epiphany, recalling Christ's transfiguration on the mountain.

Triduum (TRIH-doo-um) Latin for "three days"; the three sacred days from Maundy Thursday evening through Easter Evening, which together celebrate the unity of the paschal mystery of Christ's death and resurrection.

urn *see* ossuary.

veil Cloth placed over sacramental vessels before and after the celebration of Holy Communion.

versicles Brief lines of scripture (often from the psalms) sung or said responsively in certain rites, including daily prayer.

Vespers From the Latin for "evening"; an evening worship service of scripture readings and prayer. Also known as Evening Prayer.

vigil A liturgical service on the eve of a festival, such as the Easter Vigil.

white Liturgical color used on festivals of Christ, the weeks of Christmas and Easter, The Holy Trinity, and certain saints' days. Symbolizes joy, gladness, purity, and the light of Christ.